Advance praise for *Radical Suburbs*

"*Radical Suburbs* is a revelation. Amanda Kolson Hurley
will open your eyes to the wide diversity and rich history
of our ongoing suburban experiment. This book gives
us all a new way to understand our varied suburbias
and how to engage a serious conversation about making
them for twenty-first century life. Essential reading for
every urbanist."

—Richard Florida,
author of *The Rise of the Creative Class*

"*Radical Suburbs* overturns stereotypes about the
suburbs to show that, from the beginning, those 'little
boxes' harbored revolutionary ideas about racial and
economic inclusion, communal space, and shared
domestic labor. Amanda Kolson Hurley's illuminating
case studies show not just where we've been but where
we need to go."

—Alexandra Lange,
author of *The Design of Childhood*

RADICAL SUBURBS

To observe the *banlieue* is to observe an amphibian. End of trees, beginning of roofs, end of grass, beginning of paving stones, end of ploughed fields, beginning of shops, the end of the beaten track, the beginning of the passions, the end of the murmur of things divine, the beginning of the noise of humankind—all of this holds an extraordinary interest.

—Victor Hugo, *Les Misérables*

RADICAL SUBURBS

Experimental Living on the Fringes of the American City

Amanda Kolson Hurley

Belt Publishing

Printed in the United States of America
First edition 2019

ISBN: 978-1-948742-36-8

Belt Publishing
3143 W 33rd Street #6
Cleveland Ohio 44109
www.beltpublishing.com

Book design by Meredith Pangrace
Cover by David Wilson

CONTENTS:

INTRODUCTION

The internet has a corner for every subgroup, and for young people who are interested in urban planning, architecture, and transportation, that's a Facebook group called New Urbanist Memes for Transit-Oriented Teens. NUMTOTs, as it's known, has 130,000 members and rising (even as Facebook has become mired in successive scandals). People in the group share photos of favorite buildings or mass-transit systems, captioning them with slangy terms of endearment like "l o n g b o i" (for an extra-long train) or "BIGBOI" (for a jumbo jet). Early in 2018, an architecture student in Montréal posed a question to the group:

> Alright gang, I have a question for you that's part of a school assignment. What bothers you the most about suburban life in general?

More than 200 responses quickly followed. They included:

- The sameness of it all. The same houses in every city, the same cars in every driveway, the [same] restaurants in every plaza, the same gifts at every Christmas, the same hotels for when [you're] visiting relatives ... it's impossible to tell where you are in the country when you are in the suburbs.

- Insular communities. It's easy to go your whole life without encountering anyone who looks or acts differently than you do.

- The conflation of isolation with wealth/success. lawns. inefficient public transit. nothing interesting within walking distance unless you find minute variations in people's prefab houses interesting. no one to people watch.

- People are so much more bitter and territorial about their space (especially their fucking lawns).

- Normalized social anxiety among people my age who live there.

- Super alienating. There's no flexibility in lifestyles or housing or transit options. It's bland and placeless.

The rest of the comments mostly hewed to the same themes: architectural monotony. Geographic and social isolation, reinforcing each other in a depressing feedback loop. A culture obsessed with wealth, privacy, and status-seeking.

NUMTOTs is not representative of younger Americans overall, but still, the poll serves as a kind of Rorschach test for how people view the suburbs. And what it suggests is that the popular conception of suburbia hasn't changed much at all in fifty-odd years. Back in the early 1960s, Malvina Reynolds wrote a song called "Little Boxes," inspired by a drive past rows of lookalike pastel-hued houses in a new suburban housing tract. (Her friend Pete Seeger had a hit with the song in 1963.) Reynolds saw the cookie-cutter houses as both symbols and shapers of the conformist mindset of the people who lived in them—doctors and lawyers who aspired to nothing more than playing golf and raising children who would one day inhabit "ticky-tacky" boxes of their own.

But Reynolds was wrong about who lived in this suburb, Daly City, just south of San Francisco. It was not originally home to the martini-chuffing doctors and lawyers she imagined, but to working-class and lower-middle-class (white) strivers who were the last group to get in on the postwar housing boom. Then, only a few years after Reynolds wrote "Little Boxes," Filipinos and other immigrants from Asia began arriving in Daly City. The "ticky-tacky" architecture that Reynolds scorned proved amenable to them remodeling and expanding homes for extended families, and Daly City became the "Pinoy capital" of the U.S., with the highest concentration of immigrants from the Philippines in America.

For some reason, misinformed clichés like this one still define suburbia in the popular imagination, and it drives me crazy. I lived in Montgomery County, Maryland, outside of Washington, D.C. I'm a suburbanite, but my life doesn't revolve around manicured lawns, status anxiety, or a craving for homogeneity. My suburban experience includes riding the bus as people chat around me in Spanish and French Creole. It's living in a condo, with no yard or garage, and having neighbors who hail from Tibet, Brazil, and Kenya as well as Cincinnati. It's my son attending a school that reflects the diversity—and stubborn inequality—of America today.

"Suburbia" is a dizzyingly broad category. The term refers to semi-rural areas where strip malls nibble at farmland and those where tall towers loom over the city line. It encompasses McMansions and mobile homes, airports and light-industrial estates, landfills and parkland. More than half of all Americans live in the suburbs, and according to demographer William Frey, within the country's 100 largest metropolitan areas, more than half of blacks, Hispanics, and Asians do. Minorities now account for

35 percent of suburban residents, in line with their share of the total U.S. population. Diverse suburbs are growing faster than predominantly white suburbs. Also, increasingly, new immigrants bypass central cities and settle directly in suburbia. (In my county, for example, 33 percent of residents are foreign-born.) Suburban poverty is widespread and growing: The number of poor people in the suburbs surpassed the number in the cities during the 2000s. The 2018 midterm elections showed that suburbanites are now more likely to vote Democratic than Republican. But you wouldn't necessarily know any of this from popular culture. Pop suburbia is either a facade of upper-middle-class conformity about to crack and reveal its dark secrets—think of the movies *American Beauty* and *Little Children*—or a hellscape of dead malls and "zombie subdivisions," as chronicled obsessively by the media after the financial crash of 2008.

The emergence of the second narrative reflects an important shift in the relationship of city to suburb, suburb to city. After decades of decline, U.S. cities have made a vigorous comeback. Between 2000 and 2015, many cities grew faster than their suburbs for the first time in generations. Young, college-educated professionals poured into urban neighborhoods. Companies abandoned their verdant suburban campuses and moved downtown. City economies boomed. Cranes massed on skylines, and new apartments, offices, restaurants, bars, and coffee shops sprouted. Suburbs found themselves in the unfamiliar position of wondering where everyone had gone and what they were doing wrong.

In gentrified areas of San Francisco or Washington, D.C., young professionals might tell you that they could never live in a suburban "bubble," or complain that the suburbs are "too white"—despite those suburbs having become more diverse, racially and socioeconomically, than their own city neighborhoods. "[Difference may actually be the defining characteristic of suburbia, rather than the sameness consistently attributed to it," writes urban historian Margaret Crawford. "In fact, currently, in an inversion of conventional wisdom, cities are becoming more homogeneous while suburbs grow more diverse." Yet the stereotype of "little boxes" lives on. Misconceptions blinker our imagining of what suburbs are and might become in the future.

The way we talk about suburbia hasn't caught up with today's reality, but it's at odds with past reality, as well. This book is about waves of idealists who founded alternative suburbs outside of Eastern cities, beginning in the 1820s and continuing through the 1960s. These groups had very different backgrounds and motivations, but all of them believed in the power of the local community to shape moral and social values. As opposed to the groups who went far into America's interior to settle isolated communes, the subjects of this book were, in a paradoxical-sounding phrase, practical utopians. They were reformers, not revolutionaries. Staying close to the city let them try out new ways of living with a financial lifeline and emergency exit. The fact that their communities continue to prosper is a testament to the staying power of their ideas. At a time when—it could reasonably be argued—the future of the country hangs on what suburbs do over the next twenty or thirty years, they show that bold social and architectural experimentation is not alien to suburbia. In fact, it's our birthright.

The basic story of the suburbs that most Americans know goes something like this: Back in the nineteenth and early twentieth centuries, country retreats for the wealthy and "streetcar suburbs" popped up on the outskirts of cities. Then, after World War II, new roads and cheap government mortgages drew millions of people— white people, that is—from apartments and rowhouses in the city to freshly bulldozed suburban subdivisions. Many of them were fleeing neighborhoods and schools that African Americans had recently moved into, the destructive phenomenon known as white flight. Suburbia was where these white, middle-class Americans could isolate themselves from perceived urban ills, in a static and regulated environment where private space, property ownership, racial homogeneity, and the nuclear family were the dominant values.

This isn't untrue, but it's very far from complete. The suburb was not an American or even Western invention. Suburbs have been around as long as cities have. In the third millennium BCE, the suburbs of Ur stretched miles beyond the city. In ancient Rome, the urban outskirts were where the nobility kept "country" retreats. But this zone was also where the Romans pushed what they didn't want to see, hear, or smell—noxious industries like tanning and brickmaking, for instance. Even in the Middle Ages, city walls were not the hard boundaries they seemed to be. Suburban zones lay beyond them, and people and goods moved back and forth. "[W]alled medieval cities in Europe and elsewhere enlarged their walled areas several times to accommodate their fringe belts and to prepare for future expansion," writes the urban scholar Shlomo Angel. Prostitutes, gypsies, and lepers were often consigned to live *sub urbs*, literally "below the city" in Latin. The very term implies the height of the protective wall and the uncertain status of those outside its embrace.

In early modern England, the rapid growth of London overflowed into suburbs that were renowned for debauchery. "Suburb sinner" became a slang term for prostitute. "[T]hese suburb sinners have no lands to live upon but their legs," wrote playwright Thomas Dekker in a pamphlet of invective. London's suburbs, he claimed hyperbolically, had "[m]ore alehouses than there are taverns in all Spain and France."

Even in more recent times, suburbs were often places where settlement had outpaced the institutions of law and religion and the reach of infrastructure. In French cities during the early nineteenth century, industrial workshops sprang up in the *faubourgs*, and these areas then swelled with landless people in search of work. Lying beyond the *octroi*, or urban tax boundary, and often lacking gas lighting and regular police patrols, these neighborhoods were where you'd go for cheap wine, and maybe a brawl, on a Saturday night. They were home to prostitutes, ragpickers, peddlers, and other marginal people among a growing proletariat, and bohemians seeking a frisson of danger.

The French elite looked down on *faubourg*-dwellers as low-class. A court report from 1838 told of a Madame Dussus, sentenced to prison "for absconding with and strangling domestic animals." The poor woman had been caught selling stolen cats, "of which the wretched cooks of the faubourgs and the suburbs make excellent stews," the report noted sneeringly. Several years earlier, in Lyon, there had been an insurrection by silk workers on the fringes of that city. The high-ranking official Gaspard de Chabrol warned King Louis-Philippe of the same thing happening in Paris: "Your prefects of police are allowing the capital to be blocked by a hundred factories. Sire, this is the cord that will strangle us one day." Fear of the suburbs as a hotbed of class violence rings from his words.

The American suburb dates back further than the nineteenth century. Much further, in fact: near St. Louis, archaeologists recently found the remains of a 900-year-old suburb of Cahokia, once the largest Native American city north of Mexico. (The site of the ancient suburb is in the modern town of East St. Louis, Illinois, "halfway between a crumbling meat packing plant and a now-closed strip club," as *NPR* reported.)

As Kenneth Jackson relates in his classic history of American suburbs, *Crabgrass Frontier*, Boston, Philadelphia, and New York all had suburbs prior to the Revolutionary War. Philadelphia's first suburb, Southwark, was populated mostly by artisans and maritime workers, while the wealthy congregated in the center of town. This pattern of fashionable core versus modest outskirts was standard in the early nineteenth century. In southern cities like Savannah and New Orleans, enslaved people initially lived in humble dwellings close to the homes of their owners, but the growing practice of "living out" prompted them to move to the farthest corners of the city, beyond its official boundaries. "Thus, the first Americans to move to the suburbs for racial reasons were black, not white," Jackson writes.

The mid-nineteenth century saw the birth of the first suburbs we would recognize as such, including Frederick Law Olmsted's Riverside, Illinois, and Llewellyn Park in New Jersey, designed by Alexander Jackson Davis. These enclaves seeded the suburbs that blossomed around American cities in the late 1800s and early 1900s. They were what Robert Fishman called *Bourgeois Utopias* in his influential book by that title—the leafy realm of rich and upper-middle-class Anglo-Saxon families living in elegant Queen Anne and Tudor Revival houses. Think Chestnut Hill, Pennsylvania; the Country Club District in Kansas City, Missouri; and Beverly Hills, California. In all three of those suburbs and others, industrial and most commercial activities were banished, and blacks and Jews were prohibited from purchasing homes by restrictive covenants.

According to Fishman, suburbs built in this era "provided the model that all subsequent suburbs have attempted to imitate":

> Structurally, these suburbs were at once separate from the industrial city and yet, through the streetcar and steam railroad, easily accessible to it. Socially, they housed a powerful and self-conscious bourgeoisie that combined the old business and professional elite with the "new middle class" anxious to establish its separateness from the immigrant cities. In design, the substantial houses set in open, tree-shaded lots summed up that blend

of property, union with nature, and family life which defines the suburban tradition.

It isn't difficult to perceive the influence these archetypal suburbs continue to exert on American culture, from John Hughes' *Home Alone* (filmed in a center-hall colonial in Winnetka, Illinois, incorporated in 1869) to Celeste Ng's bestselling 2017 novel *Little Fires Everywhere* (set in Shaker Heights, Ohio, incorporated in 1912). They certainly proliferated around the country through the 1920s. But even in their heyday, they weren't the norm on the urban periphery.

The anti-urban prejudice in American life goes back to Thomas Jefferson, who famously wrote, "When we get piled upon one another in large cities, as in Europe, we shall become as corrupt as Europe," and who encouraged the creation of independent homesteads with his gridded land survey in 1785. In the mid-nineteenth century, popular writers championed the freestanding cottage in nature as the ideal American home. Ultimately, though, what inspired developers at that time to start building suburbs—and the bourgeoisie to flock to them—was not a Jeffersonian hatred of the urban, or a deep-seated preference for detached houses ensconced in greenery. It was middle-class homebuyers' desire to safeguard their investment at a time when the outskirts of cities were in wild flux. In the mid-nineteenth century, owners of villas in the farthest reaches of New York saw their property values erode as the "undesirables" of the city they'd left behind caught up with them. Frederick Law Olmsted described the phenomenon in a letter in 1860: Villas on new roads out of the city were soon joined by workshops, he wrote, drawn there by the convenient location. Along with the workshops came "cheap tenements and boarding houses," he wrote. Unsold villas were sometimes occupied by Irish squatters, who kept goats on the lawns.

The picture this summons of a volatile mix of rich and poor, mansion and shanty, is at odds with the stability that we regard as a hallmark of suburbia. Agriculture still thrived on the urban outskirts, often practiced by foreign-born and non-white farmers, while factories encroached. Shantytowns dotted the city's rim, as did no-frills developments in which people built houses on raw lots, dug wells, kept chickens and cows, and grew vegetables. In his book *Crabgrass Crucible*, on the suburbs' role in environmentalism, historian Christopher Sellers argues that these scruffy suburbs were in fact more common than the "picturesque enclaves" that became symbolic:

> Even around the richest cities, [such] enclaves were far and away the exceptions in urban-edge development. For every one of these lavishly endowed, upper-end projects, scores of other developers bought and subdivided urban-edge lands and sold them with fewer urban provisions and less artful or ornate foliage. Housing clusters and entire towns suddenly appeared over the 1880s and 1890s and were sold to "working" families of modest income.

Likewise, in his book *Unplanned Suburbs*, Richard Harris chronicles the blue-collar suburbs that were characteristic of Toronto's periphery in the early twentieth century. These were populated by recent immigrants from Britain, who built themselves shacks and simple cottages, raised farm animals, and took in lodgers to make ends meet. An illustration from the *Toronto Globe* in 1908 suggests how tenuous their circumstances could be: a man standing in front of his shack fights off a wolf, labeled "STARVATION," as his family looks on worriedly from inside. In the U.S., there were factory suburbs like Homestead, Pennsylvania, adjacent to Andrew Carnegie's U.S. Steel plant, where immigrants from Eastern Europe—including my great-grandfather—crowded into dark, narrow houses.

Not all early suburbanites were white, whether Anglo or ethnic. For one thing, residents of high-end enclaves hired black cooks and drivers and nannies, and their employees needed somewhere to live close by. (That it would be somewhere else was a given.) Working-class African Americans bought lots in subdivisions advertised in black newspapers—sometimes named for Booker T. Washington or Frederick Douglass—and built homes there. In *Places of Their Own*, historian Andrew Wiese writes at length about Chagrin Falls Park near Chagrin Falls, Ohio, an early-twentieth-century black suburb that grew to hundreds of residents, four churches, an elementary school, and a community center. Communities like Chagrin Falls Park often had unpaved roads and lacked electricity and plumbing for decades, a denial of services rooted in white racism. Suburban towns cut black enclaves out of their boundaries much the same way that federal agencies redlined black urban neighborhoods. Nevertheless, by 1960, 2.5 million African Americans had moved to the suburbs. Middle-class and elite blacks found their own footholds in (among other places) Evanston, Illinois, and on Long Island.

America's suburban stew of affluent, modest, and hardscrabble settlements—mixed with factories, farms, garbage dumps, and cemeteries—is part of a global historical pattern. But the sense of otherness has drained out of the word suburb entirely, narrowing how we speak and think about life on the edge of the city. In this book, I argue that heading for the urban fringes to live by nonconformist values is a long American tradition, and one we can learn a great deal from today.

To be sure, nonconformism has never been the dominant impulse behind suburban settlement in the United States. In the nineteenth century, a cult of domesticity took hold among the white middle class that promoted the suburban, single-family home as the bedrock of Christian virtue. Popular writers encouraged women to be industrious housekeepers and "the Angel in the House," banishing filth—biological and moral—from the family domicile and nurturing healthy, God-fearing children. In their best-selling book *The American Woman's Home*, authors Catherine Beecher and her sister Harriet Beecher Stowe (of *Uncle Tom's Cabin* fame) called the suburban dwelling "the home church of Jesus Christ." Writers of this period warned that cities were hives of vice, and some Americans feared that apartment living was degrading the morals of the young. Small apartments with shared facilities were rumored to encourage promiscuity.

But something else was stirring at the edge of the city: communes, both of the religious and secular variety. In 1776, the Shakers built their first communal village on this continent outside of Albany, New York, in what is now the suburb of Colonie, New York. In 1822, they settled what would eventually become Shaker Heights, several miles from Cleveland. Two decades later, amid a national craze for commune-building, the Inspirationists, a group of mystical Lutheran dissidents, emigrated from Germany and formed a colony just southeast of Buffalo, in West Seneca, New York. Brook Farm, a collective formed by the Transcendentalists— and probably the most famous of the nineteenth-century communes—sat in West Roxbury, Massachusetts, only nine miles from downtown Boston. (It is now within the city's limits.)

Brook Farm was short-lived, as were most manifestations of commune fever. But a few suburban communes proved surprisingly tenacious, such as the Harmonists' Economy in Pennsylvania (discussed in Chapter 1) and the anarchist colony of Stelton in New Jersey (Chapter 2). Even those that disbanded quickly helped to stir other movement. When communes failed or their inhabitants moved west, newcomers took over their houses and workshops. The historian Dolores Hayden sees direct links between these communitarian settlements and "suburbs" as we know them; some of the same people involved in socialist collectives in New Jersey, she points out, went on to design picturesque early suburbs.

While trains and streetcars fueled suburban growth in the early 1900s, a new idea seized intellectuals and prompted them to look toward the suburbs with utopia in their eyes. The Garden City was a template for a town that would blend the best of city and country, envisioned by British stenographer Ebenezer Howard (1850-1928). The pleasant, bucolic-sounding term "Garden City" and its subsequent application to all manner of suburban developments has obscured the radicalism of Howard's social aims. First, his intention was to provide dignified dwellings for all classes of society except the landed gentry, from the unskilled laborer to the upper-middle-class professional. Second, the Garden City would be a complete walkable town, not just a collection of houses, with workplaces and shops and cultural facilities. And third, the fully realized Garden City would own the land it stood on and use rent increases to fund public services. This was an attempt to reform capitalism, ridding it of the exploitation by landowners that created stark inequality. Howard saw the Garden City as a peaceful alternative to revolution.

Howard's concept inspired experiments including Forest Hills and Sunnyside Gardens in Queens—suburbs within New York City—and Greenbelt, Maryland, discussed in Chapter 3. The Garden City remained influential through and after World War II, when it fed into the New Towns movement in the United Kingdom and other European countries (and to a lesser degree, in the United States). It is possible to draw a fairly straight line from Greenbelt to Reston, Virginia, the 1960s New Town that is the subject of Chapter 6. Whereas the Garden City and New Town sought to replace the bedroom suburb with a satellite city, there was a different movement around the same time to reclaim the single-family suburban enclave for progressive ends. Chapters 4 and 5 recount the stories of Five Fields and Six Moon

Hill in Lexington, Massachusetts, and Concord Park in Trevose, Pennsylvania. Five Fields and Six Moon Hill were designed by protégés of the architect Walter Gropius to advance an egalitarian Modernism. Concord Park was a tract of "little boxes" with a radical twist—it was built by a civil rights activist for the explicit purpose of promoting racial integration.

A skeptical reader might object that most Americans don't live in intentional communities, garden cities, or houses designed by famous architects. Americans are individualists who love private property and "No Trespassing" signs, so how much can these places really teach us? Individualism is an important strand in the American character, as de Tocqueville and countless others have observed. But affiliationism is, too. The efforts chronicled in these pages to forge a better kind of community—a beacon for others and a model for future generations—have no less a precursor than the Puritans' city upon a hill.

It's true that these models didn't catch on enough to change mainstream housing and development in a meaningful way. And none performed the kind of social alchemy that was their planners' ultimate dream. Six Moon Hill and Five Fields didn't bring about truly cooperative child rearing. Greenbelt failed to redirect suburban development into walkable satellite cities. Concord Park did not make an appreciable dent in racial segregation, and Reston had to dilute its founder's vision to attract enough homebuyers to survive.

Utopia is, by definition, not achievable. But all of these experiments succeeded to a degree that may come as a surprise. They represent real, viable challenges to what can still seem like immovable pillars of suburban life: the traditional single-family home, the self-sufficient nuclear family, racial and economic segregation, and the stark separation of residential from non-residential spaces. They fostered a special identity and sense of pride that have lasted for generations.

A chicken-and-egg question runs through the book. Do people with certain values and inclinations opt into such communities, or do the communities inculcate these values in residents? The answer seems to be both. Time and again during the course of this project, people told me how much these places meant to them, and that they had shaped their lives for the better. A few had grown up in their suburbs as children, left for college and careers, and decided to come back. Others had sought out the communities they live in now because they had been raised in other unconventional suburbs. Still others found their communities appreciably different from, and superior to others nearby. In Lexington, two residents of Six Moon Hill, Peter Warren and Sandra Galejs, told me it was unlike anywhere else they had lived, and they couldn't imagine ever moving out. "I think I would be less rooted" elsewhere, Galejs said. "I didn't have a sense that my neighborhood was important before ... When I talk to other people and realize that most people don't know their neighbors, or they know them because of one border dispute or who pays for the tree that fell down, I feel really grateful."

The normative American suburb is in many ways ill-suited to how we live in the twenty-first century. It was planned around stay-at-home Mom, Dad, and little Jack and Sally, but there are now more single people, one-parent families, and multigenerational clans than nuclear families with young children. Millennials, with anemic wages and lots of student-loan debt, often can't afford the suburban split-levels they grew up in. And many of them wouldn't want to buy them if they could, anyway. It's the stuff of countless trend pieces, but Millennials really do have a preference for urban living. Polls show they value being able to walk to shops and restaurants and having short commutes. Young adults also report being happier in cities than previous generations did at the same stage in life. The market and many policymakers don't seem to have gotten the message yet. The most distant suburbs are growing fastest (because that's where it's possible to build), and the average size of a new house in the U.S. has ballooned to almost 2,600 square feet. Instead of opportunities to live in more compact homes in close-in suburbs and cities, Millennials are being offered a narrow and outdated version of the American dream.

We could be in the middle of the "Great Inversion," as the writer Alan Ehrenhalt terms it: a national shift from the postwar pattern of wealthy suburbs and poor city, back to the historic norm of elite city and downmarket suburbs. Even if we aren't, though, rising social inequality and demographic shifts—and above all climate change—make it imperative to rethink who and what our suburbs are for. Already, some suburban jurisdictions are adapting to new realities, transforming themselves into "urban 'burbs" with pedestrian downtowns, light-rail lines, and new forms of housing. This conscious urbanization is savvy in terms of meeting younger people's preferences, but it's also the only environmentally responsible course. The October 2018 report of the UN Intergovernmental Panel on Climate Change warned that we have only a short window of time—until the year 2030—to bring down emissions enough to avoid catastrophic warming, and doing so will require "rapid, far-reaching and unprecedented changes in all aspects of society." Research shows that sprawl-style land use increases greenhouse-gas emissions by decentralizing jobs and services and prompting us to drive more. People who drive everywhere are also less active and therefore more liable to chronic conditions such as diabetes. Suburbs, like cities, need many more neighborhoods where residents can meet daily needs on foot; streets that give priority to walkers, cyclists, and light rail and buses over cars; and high-quality public spaces. Retrofitting suburbia, to quote Ellen Dunham-Jones and June Williamson, who wrote a book with that title, is "the big project for this century."

Unfortunately, the suburbs carry a stigma among the very people who could improve them: architects. The design elite has alternately patronized or inveighed against suburbia for years, ever since the International Congress of Modern Architecture called the suburb "a kind of scum churning against the walls of the city" in 1933. One avant-garde architect has called suburbia "reprehensible"; a prominent New York architecture firm lists "single-family suburban homes" and "suburban subdivisions, malls and office parks" as "what we won't do" on its website. Recently, when the celebrated Italian architect Renzo Piano broke ranks to design a mall in a California suburb, it sent ripples of surprise and amusement through the design press. A number of the places described in this book exist thanks to earlier architects who ignored the derision or skepticism of colleagues. The abandonment of suburbia by leading designers has had a cost. New housing is dominated by large single-family homes in regulated HOA developments. New suburban "town centers" are internally walkable and sometimes served by public transit, but their architecture is uninspired and hokey. However, it's not just architects' fault. Zoning limits neighborhood design possibilities, and big homebuilders have achieved such economies of scale that alternatives to the Pulte or D.R. Horton home struggle to compete on price. Plus, developers of multifamily housing and mixed-use projects often assume that suburbanites have unsophisticated taste.

One of the most vocal and influential critics of suburbia today is the Belgian architect Léon Krier, known for his polemical writings and cartoons in praise of traditional urbanism. For Krier, the suburb is by definition a parasite, a malignancy. "The suburb hates itself: it knows that it is neither countryside nor city and wants to conquer the world because it cannot be at peace with itself," he has written. "The suburb strangles the city by surrounding it and kills the city, tearing out its heart. A suburb can only survive, it cannot live." To drive the point home, Krier drew a cartoon of a suburb with houses shaped like cannons, firing on the adjacent city.

Krier is wrong—for one thing, cities are more apt to swallow up their suburbs than be killed by them. But more than that, his words betray fear and revulsion at the hybrid quality of suburbia, at how it confounds the neat binaries of town and country, village and city, manmade and natural. What if we embraced that in-betweenness instead of condemning it? The epigraph of this book quotes Victor Hugo, who found "extraordinary interest" in the "amphibian" that was the nineteenth-century suburb. Part water, part dry land. Part urban, part rural. For the species on either side of it, the ecotone is a testing ground and a portal to the unfamiliar. This book celebrates the possibilities of standing on that threshold.

A NOTE ON DEFINITIONS

Attempts to define "suburb" are legion, and fraught. The U.S. Census Bureau sets clear parameters for "urban" and "rural" census tracts, but not suburban ones, leaving them up to interpretation. Academics have used various criteria to decide what makes somewhere a suburb: physical characteristics (like looping roads and detached housing); population density thresholds; residential character; a maximum distance or journey time to the central city; a newer date of settlement relative to the central city; and so on. But the word keeps wriggling away from those who want it to stand still.

Many suburbs don't look or act the way we'd expect them to. The economist Jed Kolko recently polled Americans on whether their neighborhood was urban, suburban, or rural. After correlating their responses with the population density in their zip codes, he concluded that many city neighborhoods in the United States are in fact suburban, and perceived as such by their residents. On the other side of the coin, a resident of Somerville, Massachusetts, or Evanston, Illinois, might identify as an urbanite and object to the label of suburb being applied to his or her town.

Some suburbs are larger or denser than the cities they border. Occasionally they predate those cities (for example, Alexandria, Virginia, was founded before Washington, D.C.). Some are packed with people—the suburban census tract where I used to live, in Silver Spring, Maryland, has a density of 16,000 people per square mile, higher than the average in Boston or Philadelphia. In other suburbs, people and buildings are thinly scattered. Fixing a radius around a city to mark where the countryside ends and suburbs begin can be useful, but only for so long; as development pushes outward or a transportation network expands, the radius becomes obsolete.

In this book I use a deliberately broad definition of "suburb": a community outside the municipal bounds of a large city but within commuting range and economically enmeshed with it. All six of the neighborhoods discussed in these pages are located within major metropolitan areas (as defined by the U.S. Office of Management and Budget), but outside the urban cores of those areas. The neighborhoods are all medium-density, according to a population-density index devised by *CityLab*.

Cities tend to absorb their suburbs over time. Because of annexation, today's hip urban district is often yesterday's suburb—an erstwhile retreat from the noise and grime of nineteenth-century industry. Mount Pleasant in Washington, D.C., and the brownstone neighborhoods of Brooklyn are good examples of former suburbs turned quintessentially urban. The obverse is that today's suburb is also tomorrow's city neighborhood in embryo.

This is important to bear in mind when thinking about suburbs, but for the purposes of this book, I chose to restrict my focus to places that remain municipally separate from central cities today. I had two reasons for doing so: First, most people would agree without hesitation that these locations are suburban, so explanations will not be required in each case. Second, it is more in line with the thesis of the book to discuss present-day suburbs than former suburbs that have been enfolded by the city. In the latter instance, it would be too easy to see them as destined to become "unsuburban" eventually, which would be the wrong conclusion to draw.

This is a short book, so its scope is necessarily limited. The six case studies are all in the eastern part of the U.S., which unfortunately leaves out a big part of the suburban story (past and present) and many fascinating examples in the Midwest and West. Five are located in prosperous, growing metropolitan areas, and as a consequence, the special challenges of suburbs that are losing population or experiencing economic decline are not considered fully here. Some non-normative types of suburban settlements— like company towns, military bases, and mobile-home parks—are not addressed, either. My discussion foregrounds questions of planning, design, and housing, while devoting less attention to transportation, commerce, industry, and governance. This is not meant to imply that suburbs, in the U.S. or elsewhere, are one-dimensional bedroom communities. Recent books and articles have mapped a rich spectrum of landscapes and issues, from the mid-twentieth-century corporate campus and the contested political space of suburbia in the U.S., to Soviet-era housing estates in Eastern Europe, to the fast-growing, informal outskirts of cities in the Global South. I hope readers will seek them out.

CHAPTER 1

CELIBACY AND CO-HOUSING ON THE SUBURBAN FRONTIER

Ambridge, Pennsylvania

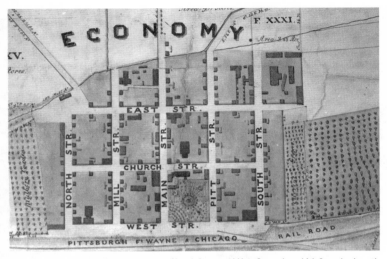

The heart of Economy was the intersection of Church Street and Main Street (now 14th Street), where the church and George Rapp's house faced each other. The formal landscaped garden was Rapp's and included a pavilion and grotto.

STILL TO BE SEEN AT ECONOMY NOW AMBRIDGE, PA. FIGURE IN CENTER AN ECONOMITE IN HER CUSTOM THE ECONOMITE HOUSES HAD NO FRONT DOORS

TYPICAL ECONOMITE HOUSE

The Baker House, with vines growing on the exterior and the door located on the side, pictured on an undated postcard.

"We are a little wild here with numberless projects of social reform," Ralph Waldo Emerson wrote in a letter to Thomas Carlyle. "Not a reading man but has a draft of a new community in his waistcoat pocket." Emerson wrote this in 1840, as the United States was entering the era of Peak Commune. Over the course of the nineteenth century, but especially in its middle decades, bands of rebels, misfits, and seekers spread all over the country, founding scores of utopian communities.

I've always loved reading about these places, which is how I learned about Economy, Pennsylvania. Economy, founded in 1824, was the heaven on earth of a German religious group called the Harmonists. It was also a proto-suburb, a stagecoach suburb[1] of Pittsburgh. A close-in location made it easier to bring in supplies, get products to market, dabble in tourism, and navigate local politics to the community's advantage. Economy was not the only such community on the fringes of a larger city. In 1822, Shakers founded the North Union settlement in northeast Ohio, near Cleveland; it later became Shaker Heights, and the lakes the Shakers created by damming a brook are now local parks. Outside of Buffalo, a German

[1] Confusingly, there is a modern-day Economy, Pennsylvania, but its boundaries do not coincide with the old town of Economy. The modern borough of Economy was created from the Harmonists' land holdings east of their town. Here I use "Economy" to mean the Harmonist town that is now part of Ambridge.

sect called the Inspirationists established a thriving colony in what is now the suburb of West Seneca, New York. (They later decamped for Iowa, where they founded the Amana Colonies and, in an unexpected turn, pioneered refrigeration.)

Economy's intact, preserved core is rare. Many communes of its era were built of wood and subsequently burned down, or else they were slowly digested by the communities that succeeded them, like West Seneca. Their near-absence in the landscape has led to historical amnesia. But these places are an important part of the suburban story. Economy is a vivid counterpoint to the idea that there was nothing happening on the fringes of cities until streetcars and then cars came along.

Driving the fourteen miles from Pittsburgh to Economy today on Route 65, you follow the same gentle curves of the river that the old road did, although the dramatic views are now filled up by houses, rails, and sprawling sheds of heavy industry, many of them now quiet. The road passes through a chain of small suburban boroughs, some bowered and others gritty; the contrast from one to another can be so sharp that you could almost point to the boundary that divides them. In Ambridge, which falls on the gritty side of the equation, you take a right on 13th Street and there it is, behind a low white fence: Old Economy Village, now run as a historic site by the state of Pennsylvania. The visitor center, a modern building bookended by imposing gables, stands a few blocks to the north.

Old Economy Village comprises six acres, a tiny fragment of the 3,000 that the Harmonists once owned in Beaver County. (A map in the visitor center shows the original estate engulfing present-day Ambridge.) Most of that acreage was farmland, vineyards, and orchards. The historic site is the core of the village, with sixteen original buildings. But dozens more Harmonist structures, some significantly altered, dot the nearby blocks.

The physical and spiritual heart of Economy in the early nineteenth century was the intersection of Store Gasse and

Kirchen Gasse (now 14th and Church Streets), one block from the bluff overlooking the river. The most important buildings of the Harmony Society huddled here: the church, the houses of the group's leader and his son, and the Feast House, where the whole village dined together on holidays. From this corner, wide, paved streets issued at right angles, studded with Harmonist dwellings and public facilities such as the granary, the store, the doctor's office, the school, and the bake house. The pervasive use of red brick suggests cohesiveness, but on closer inspection, Economy's architecture is an odd mix of the German Baroque, Palladian, and Federal styles.

The name chosen for the town signified not industriousness or thrift (although the Harmonists had plenty of both), but "divine economy," a sense of well-managed order bent to holy purposes. The town's careful plan expressed this virtue while fostering it in the hearts and hands of residents. As the historian Karl Arndt wrote, Economy was designed to be "a city in which God would dwell among men, a city in which perfection in all things was to be attained."

Formal gardens sat above the river on the western edge of town, while the piggeries and most of the stables stood off to the east. Industrial buildings dotted the village's northern and southern edges, pottery shops and the tannery to the north, the wool factory and dye shop to the south. The Harmonists practiced a basic and sensible form of zoning, keeping noisome factories and barns well away from the society's most vital and symbolic buildings and members' homes. Water was supplied from the hills to the east through pipes of hollowed logs, which fed several pumps in town.

On the day of my family's visit, a guide named Sandy, dressed in the Harmonist uniform of a bell-shaped dark-blue skirt and matching bonnet, showed us inside the Baker House, staged to represent a typical dwelling. At its peak, the town had more than 100 houses exactly like this one, a two-story brick structure with a chimney rising from the ridge of its gabled roof, and with the door on the side, not the front, of the house. The house was small and neat inside: two rooms downstairs and two up, plus a one-story sleeping porch added by the Harmonists somewhat later than the house's construction in the late 1820s. As was typical of Harmonist structures, its outer walls were (and still are) trellised with grapevines; the heat absorbed by the bricks warms the grapes to produce sweeter fruit, which the Harmonists used to make wine.

Between six and eight people shared each house. Often they were related by blood or marriage, but sometimes not; single adults roomed with other single people or married couples. This setup was feasible, even in a very small house lacking privacy, for one reason: the Harmonists were mostly celibate.

In 1807, before the founding of Economy, the Harmonists experienced a religious revival. From that point on, they renounced sex. Husbands and wives continued to live together, but were expected to do so as brother and sister. The number of births declined sharply, although records show that children were still born. (Clearly, for some, the flesh was weaker than the will.)

"Of the six to eight people who lived [in a Harmonist house], one would be chosen as the housekeeper, usually a woman," Sandy, a petite, chatty woman with pale blue eyes, told us. "She was like a typical Fifties stay-at-home mom." The housekeeper did all the cooking; the other members of the household went off to work in the factories or fields, but were still close enough to home that they returned for lunch.

Each house had its own root cellar (under a trap door in the lower floor), chicken shed, and outhouse. There were eight houses to a block, and each block shared a half-acre for growing vegetables and herbs, a water pump, and a bake oven. The shared ovens were eventually replaced by a central bakery serving the whole village.

In a corner of the kitchen at the Baker House stood a stone sink, plain and durable, not much to look at. In fact, it was part of a cleverly engineered public-works system. The sink once drained into a covered barrel outside the house. When full, the barrel was taken to the piggery, and the dirty dishwater was mixed with the pigs' slop. Not only did this recycle water and prevent yards from becoming mucky, it made the slops more appetizing to the pigs and even wormed them, thanks to the lye soap the Harmonists used to wash dishes. "The whole process was an admirable combination of domestic science, sanitary engineering, and veterinary medicine," according to one historian.

That a village in western Pennsylvania should have such infrastructure stunned observers in the 1820s and early 1830s. Pittsburgh then was a frontier city of only 10,000 souls, yet an obscure German preacher managed to achieve a level of comfort and cleanliness that residents of great cities might envy.

Who were the people who arrived in the Pennsylvania wilderness and constructed a handsome, bustling, six-block-by-three-block testament to "divine economy" in a matter of months? They were Pietists, part of a movement within Lutheranism that emphasized the living of a devout life and direct study of the Bible over orthodox religious doctrine. Many of them had come to America in 1804, after being persecuted by the authorities in Wurttemberg, a territory of the Holy Roman Empire (now southwestern Germany). Their leader was a man named Johann Georg Rapp.

Born in 1757, Rapp grew up in the village of Iptingen, about twenty miles from Stuttgart. An intelligent boy from a peasant family, he completed basic schooling and took up farm work, weaving, and the Bible. Coming to believe that the Lutheran Church was not the true church, he stopped attending services and began reading from the Bible with friends and neighbors. These gatherings grew, and Rapp came under suspicion as a threat to the social order. In 1803, after years of trouble with the authorities, he urged his congregation to follow him to America.

Rapp was forty-six years old and spoke hardly any English, but he and a few other men went ahead to find a suitable tract of land. After traveling in Pennsylvania, Ohio, and Maryland, Rapp bought land in Butler County in western Pennsylvania in December 1804. Meanwhile, several ships of Pietists had arrived in Baltimore and Philadelphia.

Two months later, Rapp and nearly 500 of his followers established the Harmony Society, all signing legally binding agreements called articles of association. These short and straightforward documents didn't touch on their shared religious beliefs, but they clearly laid out how the Harmonists pledged to live together in the New World:

- Each member would hand over his or her possessions "for the benefit and use of the congregation," and would not expect payment for work performed while part of the society.

- In return, members and their children would receive "necessary instruction in church and school" from the society, as well as lodging, food and drink, clothing, and care in their sickness and old age.

- Members would show "due and ready obedience" toward those appointed as the society's leaders, and would endeavor to promote the good of the whole society.

- Members wishing to leave the society would be refunded their original property, or, if they had been poor, would receive a cash donation on departure.

Thirteen years before Karl Marx was born (in Trier, another city in southwestern Germany), these German Pietist émigrés organized their small society along communist lines. They wanted to return to the ways of the early church, as described in the Book of Acts: "All who believed were together and had all things in common; they would sell their possessions and goods and distribute the proceeds to all, as any had need."

Their first settlement was Harmony, Pennsylvania, about twenty miles north of Economy. They toughed out a winter in log cabins and built a grist mill, and Harmony grew into a prosperous village of 800 by 1811. However, Rapp felt their tract was too small to support the perfect community he sought, and the winters were too long and harsh for raising grapevines, which many of the society's members (including Rapp) had done with skill back in Germany.

In 1814, the society put Harmony up for sale and decamped in phases to Indiana. There, beside the Wabash River, they founded New Harmony. Although the land here was fertile, many Harmonists contracted fever, and their English-speaking neighbors were cool toward the German newcomers. Yet over the next decade, they built a town with broad streets, busy factories, two fine churches, and a pleasure garden with a labyrinth, all swathed by vineyards and orchards.

Through reports published by visitors, New Harmony, Indiana, became a point of curiosity among the American and British public, and the Harmonists' financial success attracted the notice of economists. But the Rapps seem to have felt isolated from the East and conspicuous as German-speakers in Indiana. They determined to return to Pennsylvania. In 1824, they sold New Harmony to Robert Owen, a Welsh industrialist who planned to remake it as a secular, egalitarian "village of unity and mutual cooperation." Owen's experiment was a disaster, lasting only two years; nevertheless, his failure at New Harmony is much better known than the smooth-running model town that preceded it.

That may be because, in the twenty-first century, the Harmonist belief system is hard to grasp. Rapp's followers shared a fervent conviction that the Second Coming of Christ was imminent. They believed He would first come to North America, then drive out the evil that had seized Europe, and finally bring about the Millennium in Jerusalem. The goods and money the Harmonists saved through their labor was not just a hedge against bad harvests and natural disasters; it was also preparation for the time when they would sail for Jerusalem en masse to join the Kingdom of God.

Then there's the fact of their celibacy. "The big thing people talk about [today] is the celibacy," Sarah Buffington, the curator of Old Economy Village, told me. "They just can't believe they were celibate. That's what a lot of people get stuck on."

In fact, the Harmonists' faith was less harsh and more complex than it first appears. It contained a heavy dose of mysticism. It wove in esoteric strands of Christianity, such as Rosicrucianism, which held that there was a secret spiritual and physical order to the universe that could be gleaned through advanced learning. The Harmony Society's symbol was a golden rose, likely inspired by the Rosicrucians, and George Rapp performed experiments in alchemy, the tradition of attempting to turn base metals into gold.

The most surprising aspect of the Harmonist creed was that they worshipped Jesus as a dual being, male and female at once. Adam, they believed, was originally a dual being, whose female component was divine wisdom, or Sophia. At the Fall, Adam relinquished this spiritual Sophia for physical Eve, making futile attempts at unity through sexual congress. Man and woman would be restored to a dual state at the Second Coming, George Rapp believed. So for his followers, embracing celibacy was a form of holy preparation.

In some ways (not least their interpretation of the Bible), the Harmonists could be described as radical. They practiced communalism with great success for decades, ensuring a very decent—if by no means luxurious—quality of life for all members of the society. When they needed clothing or meat, they simply went to the store to collect them. Contemporaries were apt to note that they lived to a ripe old age. The general high standard of sanitation and provision of medical care surely played a part in this. Women learned to read, worked outside the home, and voted on society matters, and since no one received cash payment for their work, women were "paid" at the same rate as men.

Today, it is easy to underestimate the hardships that faced settlers on the American frontier in the first years of the nineteenth century. Setting up a remote homestead with only one's family, or a few others, required every person to perform countless roles: farmer, builder, carpenter, teacher, doctor, cook, security guard. Supplies from outside might be a day's journey away. Sickness was often fatal, and women died in childbirth with terrible regularity. By pooling their goods and, just as importantly, their skills, the Harmonists were able to draw on vast practical knowledge to build and run their villages, mitigating the risks of settling on the frontier, and avoiding the worst privations. With men of various trades in their number, and women unshadowed by the physical dangers of childbirth, they enjoyed relative comfort, personal safety, a steady supply of food, and the services of a doctor on site—to say nothing of music, books, companionship, and a rich spiritual life.

Their success was highlighted by none other than Friedrich Engels, who in an 1844 essay cited Economy as proof that communism was not just nice in theory but possible—desirable, even—in practice. After a lengthy description of the Harmonists and other contemporary societies in America that held property in common, he concluded: "The Americans are tired of continuing as the slaves of the few rich men who feed on the labor of the people; and it is obvious that with the great energy and endurance of this nation, community of goods will soon be introduced over a significant part of their country."

Of course, this did not come to pass. Private property-holding became more firmly entrenched in the United States. But Rapp's experiment outside of Pittsburgh was one small seed of the revolution that would later sweep through other parts of the world.

––––––––––––

Economy was not a suburb in the contemporary sense of that word. It didn't spring up in the path of the railroad or a freeway, or follow a wave of sprawl rippling out from Pittsburgh (that would come later). It was indisputably a country village, separated from Pittsburgh by a ribbon of wilderness. And that was part of its appeal, as George Rapp acknowledged in a letter to his adopted son, Frederick, soon after its founding. (Frederick was still wrapping up their affairs in Indiana.) "Here we live in the forest where thousands of hickory trees and oaks surround us and obstruct the view and where our houses stand invisible in the wilds and in the shade, invisible to people at a distance," the elder Rapp wrote.

The Harmonists, historian Arndt wrote, saw themselves as "in the world but not of it." A degree of isolation was necessary for them to live undisturbed according to their beliefs. In practical terms, they needed enough raw territory to sustain an agro-industrial fellowship of several hundred people, and a tract of several thousand acres was more readily found, and more cheaply bought, at some distance from the city. Plus, keeping civilization at arm's length meant less interference from nosy neighbors and officials.

Yet the Harmonists' separatist experiment was enmeshed with the outside world, however doomed that world might be in the eyes of the "Economites" (as other Pennsylvanians called them). Proximity to Pittsburgh supported the high standard of living that visitors marveled at. The Rapps elder and junior both took an active interest in the affairs of the world, Frederick, especially. He was the society's business leader, the CFO to his father's CEO role. (A stonemason by trade, Frederick also served as architect for the three towns, a job he performed with considerable energy and skill despite his lack of formal architectural training.) Frederick traveled frequently and maintained correspondence with the society's commercial agent in Pittsburgh and other businessmen in and beyond the state.

For the Harmonists, Pittsburgh offered both the technology of industrial prowess—it was the source of much of their state-of-the-art machinery—and a market eager to receive the goods they produced. "The vicinity to Pittsburgh, and cheap water communication, encouraged them in manufacturing," noted journalist Charles Nordhoff. Nordhoff, who made a grand tour of American utopias and chronicled it in an 1875 book, *The Communistic Societies of the United States*, visited the town a few decades after its prime. Economy came to dominate cloth manufacturing in western Pennsylvania so much that competitors accused the Rapps of creating a monopoly.

Economy shows how intertwined cities and suburbs were even before the railroad age. Its nearness to Pittsburgh buoyed the outlying town in other ways. With its picturesque setting, half-German architecture, and exotic inhabitants, who spoke a Swabian dialect of German and dressed alike in dark blue, Economy became a tourist attraction. People came to its museum, the second purpose-built museum in the entire country, paying ten cents to view taxidermied animals, rare minerals, and a clumsy portrait of Martin Van Buren. (A portion of the collection has been reassembled on site, and visitors are greeted by a stuffed buck with fearsome antlers and a black bear on the prowl.) West of the church, a substantial hotel—later demolished—welcomed guests. The hotel hosted long-distance travelers as well as day-trippers and business associates of the Rapps. The Economy Hotel, wrote Nordhoff,

> was once, before the days of the railroads, a favorite stopping-place on one of the main stage routes out of Pittsburgh; in the well-built stable and barns opposite

there was room for twenty or thirty horses; the dining-room would seat a hundred people; and here during many years was a favorite winter as well as summer resort for Pittsburghers, and an important source of income to the Economists.

Even the town's plan and architecture suggest circumspection about being "in the world" much more than at Harmony or New Harmony. Those towns had central squares, but Economy lacks one, and houses' main doors opened onto side yards rather than the street. "Harmonist life was not to be held open for the amusement of profane visitors," notes art historian Michael J. Lewis. "Instead, civic and market functions of a town square were now served by specialized buildings, with rooms for private assembly." In Indiana, the society had built a large communal dwelling similar to those of the Shakers, but it soon switched back to small two-story houses. Whatever the reason for that (maybe members preferred living in smaller groups), the houses of Economy presented a morally conventional face to the eyes of outsiders.

Up until his death in 1847, George Rapp remained the effective CEO of the Harmony Society and the unelected mayor of Economy. During this period, the Harmony Society amassed great wealth, much of which Rapp secreted away inside and even under his house, in a vault. Through the end of the nineteenth century, the Harmonists maintained their German Pietist way of life.

As the Industrial Revolution awakened in other parts of the country, Economy—with fewer and fewer able-bodied workers—lost its manufacturing edge. In the 1860s, the society founded a new town nearby, Beaver Falls, where it employed outside workers to make cutlery. The trustees who took over from the Rapps (Frederick died in 1834) invested in oil, lumber, and railroads, with handsome returns. At its peak, the Harmony Society was worth tens of millions of dollars. Much of that fortune was squandered by the last trustee, John Duss, a band master and composer with grandiose ambitions. In 1902, after a legal battle and with only eight members of the society left, Duss sold much of Economy to J.P. Morgan's American Bridge Company and its real-estate affiliate, for a factory and company town. The following year, Duss took the society's band to New York, where he rented out Madison Square Garden and spent $100,000 of Harmonist funds to turn it into a replica of Venice, complete with canals and gondoliers. The Harmony Society was finally dissolved in 1905.

Ambridge (a contraction of "American Bridge") swelled to 20,000 people in the 1920s, when it made steel used in the Chrysler Building and San Francisco–Oakland Bay Bridge, then shrank amid the general contraction of American industry in the later part of the twentieth century. U.S. Steel, the parent company of American Bridge, closed its Ambridge plant in 1984. Those jobs mostly disappeared, along with the social fabric and safety nets the unions provided.

Ambridge now struggles with a high poverty rate. But some residents see a chance for revival in the physical footprint of the Harmonist town and the factory suburb that succeeded it. The larger historic district surrounding Old Economy Village has new antique stores and a B&B, and as one booster told the local paper in June 2018, "an air of excitement." The B&B owner told the paper that one of his guests fell in love with Ambridge and moved there, because "[s]he wanted an urban setting without paying the urban prices of Pittsburgh ... She can walk, go to a store, ride a bike." A community theater opened on the other side of town in the summer of 2018. Ambridge is valuing anew its relative urbanity, as young Americans' preferences tilt from driving to walking.

That's not to deny that Economy, as a model for the twenty-first century, has many serious drawbacks. Although undeniably charismatic, George Rapp ruled as an authoritarian. (One German-speaking visitor to Economy witnessed Rapp hurling curses at society members who displeased him.) Rapp and his relatives lived well, in stately houses kitted out with china and carpets, while ordinary society members lived simply. Whether or not he was conscious of it, the vow to celibacy was a means for Rapp to hold onto power—family bonds were the biggest existential threat to his control. That threat became more than existential in 1831, when a mysterious figure named Count Leon appeared in Economy and wooed away one-third of the town's inhabitants to start a new colony nearby where marriage would be sanctioned. Leon was really a charlatan named Bernhard Muller, and the new colony soon foundered. Economy survived the schism but, historians argue, never fully recovered.

Celibacy was a slow death sentence for the Harmonist Society, as it was for the Shakers. Paradoxically, though, the rigidity it imposed is what kept the society together for so many decades. As many commentators on utopian experiments have noted, religious ones tend to fare better, because of the shared sense of identity, mission, and sacrifice. (However, there are exceptions to that rule, as we will see in the next chapter.)

I looked for a modern answer to the Harmonists, and found it in Evanston, Illinois, just north of Chicago. Reba Place Fellowship (RPF) is a Mennonite intentional community. It was founded in 1957, and its "driving vision … was to live out a life of radical Christian discipleship," according to the group's website. That meant returning to the ways of the early church, as described in the Book of Acts. Today, Reba Place members live in shared households in Evanston (and in Chicago's Rogers Park), and take part in the "common purse"—that is, they pool their incomes and hold major goods in common.

Reba Place has different levels of fellowship: only long-term "covenant members" join the common purse. (This is to prevent novices from making a hasty decision they may come to regret.) But non-covenant members can live in community if they choose to, and some do. Unlike at Economy, decisions at RPF are made by consensus. It is a democratic community, with no George Rapp at the helm.

David Hovde, RPF's public liaison, has lived in one of its Evanston households since the 1990s. Hovde currently shares a house with 10 other people, who range in age from 90-something to thirty-something. They eat almost every meal together. Hovde is a full-time caregiver for a member of his household who has muscular dystrophy. His salary, from a home-care agency, goes into the common purse, which covers the cost of his housing, food, and transportation. (The Fellowship maintains a fleet of cars.) All covenant members get a small allowance to cover their incidentals.

Hovde told me the arrangement "takes away a lot of the anxieties and worries of life" for him, and that living this way has helped him form strong bonds with people of a shared faith. "I'm very appreciative of this life, and I'm glad I found it. Life before was lonely," he said. "My family moved around quite a bit. I did not feel like I had a home base. Not everyone feels called to this way of life, and not everyone who comes here feels like this is where they should stay. But a number of us [do], and we're grateful."

With the common purse and shared households, Reba Place represents one end of the spectrum of intentional communities. Closer to the other end is the model known as co-housing, in which people live in their own homes but share certain spaces and responsibilities. Co-housing has blossomed in the United States over the last few decades, and there are now about 160 "cohos" (most of them secular) around the country. Usually, they take the form of 10 to 40 housing units surrounding a shared plaza or yard. They may also include a community kitchen for shared meals, a music rehearsal/performance space, or other common rooms. It is not so different from Economy, with its shared bread ovens, its community kitchen and barrel-vaulted Feast Hall used on religious holidays, and its music room where the society band regularly practiced.

Co-housing began in Denmark in the 1960s, and now roughly one in one hundred Danes lives in such a community. Even with the surge of interest in co-housing, it remains a fringe option in America. In terms of time and effort, the barrier to entry is high: would-be co-housers must acquire land and find a developer, or hire architects and other consultants themselves. They usually have to provide a large amount of cash upfront. And if they want sustainable features, as many do, those cost more than conventional building, with a slow payback.

But co-housing has the potential to improve lives and reduce environmental harm—especially in today's suburbia. It fosters the companionship and sense of social support that keeps loneliness at bay (and loneliness, we've learned, is a real risk to our health, especially as we age). Co-housers do chores or run errands for a friend laid up with an illness. They cook casseroles for parents busy with a new baby, and drive older neighbors to the doctor's office. Because co-housing units tend to be much smaller than the average single-family home, and are either stacked (if apartments) or tightly clustered (if townhouses or cottages), they use land very efficiently. They can also help a suburban neighborhood reach the level of density needed to support public transit, local shops, and other amenities, so driving becomes less necessary.

Rural or small-town co-housing is an attractive option for retirees. However, suburban cohos encourage age diversity, since they're closer to the job centers that working people depend on. And suburbs are more likely than city centers to offer big-enough, cheap (or at least cheaper) plots of land. The first dedicated co-housing community in America, Muir Commons, was built in Davis, California, a suburb of Sacramento, in 1991. Co-housing and co-ops aren't for everyone. But there's no good reason that one in one hundred Americans couldn't live in co-housing like the Danes if we got serious about bringing down the barriers.

When I asked Buffington, the curator at Old Economy Village, what the Harmonists can teach us today, she was quick to answer. "Work together. Work things out. Keep God at the center of everything," she said. Intentional communities are living examples of those lessons. Those that are grounded in faith, like Reba Place, exist to honor God. In secular cohos and co-living groups, a value such as social justice or ecological stewardship may be central instead, providing some of the social "glue" that religion does. As I write, a thirty-home coho of townhouses and apartments is being built in another Sacramento suburb, Fair Oaks. "Young folks have mentors, older folks have support," its website promises. That's what many of us want, whatever our backgrounds or religious beliefs.

CHAPTER 2

THE ANARCHISTS WHO TOOK THE COMMUTER TRAIN

The Stelton Colony, Piscataway, New Jersey

Stelton Modern School teachers' meeting in 1920

If an appropriate motto for Economy was "Work together. Work things out. Keep God at the center of everything," the best motto for the Stelton colony in central New Jersey might have been: "Work together. Argue it out. Keep children at the center of everything." Stelton, founded in 1915, could not have looked more different from the meticulously planned Economy. Humble cottages (some little more than shacks) ranged over a 140-acre tract of scrubland a few miles north of New Brunswick. The smattering of public buildings could have all fit inside the Harmonists' Feast Hall. Rather than a refuge for a devout religious sect, Stelton was a hive of political radicals, where federal agents came snooping during the Red Scare of 1919-1920. But it was also a suburb, a community of people who moved out of the city for the sake of their children's education and to enjoy a little land and peace. They were not even the first people to come to the area with the same idea: There was already a German socialist enclave nearby, called Fellowship Farm.

The founders of Stelton were anarchists. In the twenty-first century, the word "anarchism" evokes images of masked antifa facing off against neo-Nazis. What it meant in the early twentieth century was different, and not easily defined. The anarchist movement emerged in the mid-nineteenth century alongside Marxism, and the two were allied for a time before a decisive split in 1872. Anarchist leader Mikhail Bakunin rejected the authority of any state—even a worker-led state, as Marx envisioned—and therefore urged abstention from political engagement. Engels railed against this as a "swindle." Presumably, he would not have looked upon Stelton as kindly as he did on Economy.

But anarchism was less a coherent, unified ideology than a spectrum of overlapping beliefs, especially in the United States. Although some anarchists used violence to achieve their ends, like Leon Czolgosz, who assassinated President William McKinley in 1901, others opposed it. Many of the colonists at Stelton were influenced by the anarcho-pacifism of Leo Tolstoy and by the land-tax theory of Henry George. The most venerated hero was probably the Russian scientist-philosopher Peter Kropotkin, who argued that voluntary cooperation ("mutual aid") was a fundamental drive of animals and humans, and opposed centralized government and state laws in favor of small, self-governing, voluntary associations such as communes and co-ops.

The Stelton colony revolved around its school, the Modern School. Leaders believed that education could free the young from fear and dogma. "We claim for the Modern School," wrote colony co-founder Harry Kelly, "that the hope of the future lies in the ability of the rising generation to think and act independently without regard to the prejudices of the past." It followed a theory of education not dissimilar from today's "unschooling" movement. Arts and crafts was a main focus. The school's longtime co-principals, Elizabeth and Alexis Ferm, believed that the best kind of education for a child was creative, active, and above all, self-directed. There were no formal hours or set lessons: school was life, life was school. A printer named Joseph Ishill had come to Stelton right after its founding and taught the children to set type and print on his old hand press. Under the Ferms, pupils continued to print their own magazine, *Voice of the Children*, and also did carpentry, weaving, pottery, and metal work. Each morning began with a song-and-dance circle, "Aunty" Ferm accompanying the children on the piano.

Jon Thoreau Scott grew up in Stelton in the 1930s and '40s. He didn't learn to read until he was ten, but went on to become a professor of atmospheric science. "You could learn to read whenever you wanted to, you could play all day if you wanted to," he told me. "You could go out and play in the brook, which is what I did. Ice skating, sled riding, hiking, swimming … That was the way it went."

———————————

Heading to Stelton for the first time from my home in Maryland on a summer day, I cruised up the New Jersey Turnpike. The closer I got to New York, stands of pine trees gave way to warehouses, vast troughs of commerce where tractor-trailers lined up to feed. A few miles past the Joyce Kilmer Service Area, I turned off onto Route 18, following the curve of the Raritan River through New Brunswick. After skirting the campus of Rutgers University, the road crosses the river; then I forked right, onto Metlars Lane. I took another right onto Suttons Lane, passing a giant Rutgers parking lot topped by a canopy of solar panels, and saw the sign for School Street, once the spine of the Stelton colony.

School Street takes a dramatic couple of twists past a daycare center and around a cluster of modest vinyl-sided townhouses. Out of the corner of my eye, as I turned the wheel left and then right, I could already see what I'd come for. Two small houses—cottages, really—flicked by. The first was freshly stuccoed, but unmistakable for its boxy form and flat roof. The other was so unusual that I stopped and parked on the muddy verge of the road, which by this point had narrowed into a country lane.

The window frames of the cottage were filigreed in patterns reminiscent of Art Nouveau, and some were painted a deep blue. The plaster on the walls had been sculpted into decorative reliefs. As I approached on foot, I could make them out: stylized flowers, a swan, and a man and woman in peasant clothes, he with an axe slung over his shoulder, both gazing hopefully into the distance. This was definitely Stelton. Where else in suburbia would you find this?

The cottage was once the home of Sam Goldman, a Russian Jewish painter and decorator, and his wife, Gusta, who ran a small dairy business on the property, selling raw milk and homemade cheese and butter. The house is still owned by Leo Goldman, Sam and Gusta's younger son. "Jon Scott [the former science professor] was my best friend," he recalled of his childhood. "His father was strictly anarchist, where my father was Communist. The parents didn't get along, but Jon and I did. We did our thing." Leo Goldman's middle name is October; it was supposed to be October Revolution, but, he explained, "They wouldn't allow my mother to put Revolution on the birth certificate, so it's just October."

Most of the Stelton colonists had originally met at the Ferrer Center, an anarchist association in New York. It was named for the Catalonian anarchist and educator Francisco Ferrer, who had set up a famous democratic school—*la Escuela Moderna*—in Barcelona and was executed by the Spanish authorities in 1909. Emma Goldman, the legendary anarchist firebrand "Red Emma," was the guiding force behind the center, which hosted adult classes and lectures by the likes of Scopes-trial lawyer Clarence Darrow. In 1911, the Ferrer Center started a school for working-class children along the same lines as its namesake's, first on East Twelfth Street on the Lower East Side of Manhattan and later in Harlem.

Then, in July 1914, a bomb exploded in a tenement on Lexington Avenue, killing the four young people who had been planning to use it. (The bomb was apparently intended for John D. Rockefeller.) Three of the bombers turned out to be regulars at the Ferrer Center.

Scrutiny of the anarchists intensified, and police began to infiltrate their meetings. The center's leaders worried about the militants among their group poisoning the atmosphere for the children. Kelly and his colleague Leonard Abbott wrote in 1914, "The agitation which is carried on by the [Ferrer] Association is both necessary and desirable. But it is possible such activity may have a harmful effect on the children and warp their minds; children require brightness and joy and they can best receive that far, and yet not too far, from the 'madding crowd.'" So it was resolved to find somewhere quieter, away from spying eyes. Somewhere far, yet not too far.

The Ferrer Association purchased a tract of land in central New Jersey for $100 an acre. (Harry Kelly had learned of the area from a former girlfriend who was living at the adjacent commune, Fellowship Farm.) The association then sold one- and two-acre lots to individuals for $150 per acre, using the surplus to set aside a large plot for the school and infrastructure (like water supply). On a wet morning in May 1915, more than 100 people stepped off the train from Manhattan at the Pennsylvania Railroad's Stelton Station. They slogged a mile and half through the mud to reach their new home, which consisted of a dilapidated farmhouse, a barn, and an unfinished dormitory building. After a dedication ceremony, most people departed, leaving a small cadre of adults and children to tough it out as settlers. They started fixing up the farmhouse, laying out streets, building themselves dwellings, and planting gardens.

Within the colony's first several months, three principals of the school came and went, at least one of them put off by the primitive conditions. In the winter, it was so cold that students huddled under blankets as they ate. But under the fourth principal, the school—and the community—started to find its footing. By 1920, there were almost 150 adults and children living at Stelton year-round, and twice as many during the summer months.

Today, despite a few jutting McMansions and a row of electricity pylons near the brook, you can sense how idyllic this place must have seemed to long-ago children as they tromped over the fields, tanned and barefoot. Scott compiled a book of reminiscences by former students that brings daily life at the colony into vivid focus. Kids would climb trees to pick fruit or knock over abandoned shacks and outhouses when they were bored. Colonists kept cows, chickens, rabbits, and bees on their land. The unofficial "mayor" of Stelton was the bushy-bearded Hippolyte Havel, a legendary Czech anarchist who was a friend of Emma Goldman and playwright Eugene O'Neill. Formerly a writer, activist, and barfly in Greenwich Village, Havel lived out his old age reading and drinking in an apartment attached to the Kropotkin Library.

In Stelton's heyday, a bulletin board at the corner of School and Water Streets listed goings-on: births, deaths, political meetings, and Russian-language movies playing at the Europa, a European movie theater in New Brunswick. Some colonists took in boarders—often Modern School pupils whose parents had stayed back in New York or Philadelphia, but sometimes single men or even other families. (Finished living space was at a premium, especially during the Depression, when many summer residents chose to live at Stelton full-time because it was cheaper than the city.) The memory book reveals that it was not unusual for colonists to swap partners or to leave for a period and return with someone new. Husbands and wives were not always legally married. But colonists gossiped about the few women who raised children without a father around. When a sun-worshipping lady paraded around stark naked, neighbors asked her to knock it off. They were not *that* free-thinking.

Unlike many intentional communities, Stelton did not require any initiation or commitment. It was a participatory democracy with no formal leadership, where matters were decided by voting—one person, one vote (children included). Arguments would rage among various factions, especially between anarchists and Communists after the Russian Revolution. But since there was no coercion, disgruntled residents were free to leave whenever they chose. There were always people coming and going, including "normies" who had radical relatives or had married into anarchist families.

But that it was its own, slightly unreal world became tangible as I riffled through a folder of old photos in the archives at Rutgers University. In one photo, taken in 1924 or 1925, a group of young girls, their hair bobbed, dance through a field in drapey tunics, Isadora Duncan-style. In another, dating to 1918, two women grip either end of a length of lumber, apparently building a house. Another undated photo shows a small child playing a violin in front of a small shack, a row of sunflowers reaching as high as the roof.

Many of the colony's children stayed at the Modern School for a few years, then went on to local public schools for a more formal education. A woman named Rose Murray, now a resident of Highland Park, New Jersey, grew up in the area in the '40s. Murray would ride her bike past the colony. She didn't interact much with its residents, she said: "They were really thought of as Communists." But Stelton did influence the course of her life in a significant way. It stemmed from a playground conversation with a Stelton boy at their elementary school.

"I was in about second grade; third, tops," she remembered. "We got to talking about God, and he said, 'There's no God.' I said, 'There's no God?' So I go home and tell my mother, who's Irish Catholic. I was yanked out of that school so fast my head spun, and she sent me to a Catholic school in Highland Park."

Steltonites didn't hide their radicalism, raising a red flag on the water tower (which angry locals climbed up and tore down) after the November Revolution in Germany at the end of World War I, and sometimes refusing to stand for the national anthem at the movie theater in New Brunswick. But leafing through the documents in the archives and a book of memories compiled by Scott, another side of the colony begins to emerge. Stelton was bohemian, unorthodox. It was also suburban.

In some of the experimental communities that spread across the United States during the nineteenth century, utopians strove to live entirely off the land. This was never the goal at Stelton, although as anarchists they prized self-sufficiency. Some residents, like Goldman's mother and Scott's father, enjoyed farming their smallholdings. Goldman's parents were both from *shtetls* near cities of the Russian Empire—Minsk in her case, Kiev in his—so it may have seemed natural to settle in the semi-rural fringes of New York. But most colonists were city people who did not know how to farm and, with no other sources of income, they had to hold down jobs. They were working-class or lower-middle-class, and could not have stuck it out in central New Jersey otherwise.

On weekdays, before dawn, dozens of men and a few women piled into a red bus with the words "Stelton Cooperative Bus Ass'n" painted on the side. They bounced over pitted roads to the station, where they boarded the 5:45, arguing about politics in English and Yiddish. The conductor on the Pennsylvania Railway knew to expect them, and one can only guess what the other passengers made of the talkative, scruffy anarchists. Once in Manhattan, they headed to their jobs, mostly in the garment industry, but also as machinists, carpenters, cigarmakers, and sign-painters.

In 1919, the *New York Tribune* sent a reporter to scope out the curious settlement. Under the headline "An Anarchist Colony 70 Minutes From Broadway," the article painted Kelly as a humorless zealot, and noted the lack of order and bare facilities at the school. "Some of the anarchists who live at Stelton," the reporter noted, "commute daily to and from New York. Upon a train your anarchist is inconspicuously dressed, unless it be that he is rather below the sartorial average of the suburban traveller."

Bill Giacalone, an artist who grew up at Stelton, remembers his father, who worked as a painter in New York, riding his motorcycle to the station in the mornings. Goldman recalled: "Some people used to take two crates of eggs to New York every day. They would sell the eggs, and they made enough to pay their fare and make a living at it." The memory book mentions a woman who commuted to a dress factory in New York for a year when her husband was too sick to work. Having a school on-site and a constant adult presence in the neighborhood gave mothers more freedom of movement than was customary at the time.

Scott estimates that one-third to one-half of adult residents commuted into the city when he was a boy. Those who didn't go into New York found jobs in New Brunswick or set up shop at home. Additionally, for a time, residents ran a number of co-ops in the colony itself: a grocery, a credit union, an ice-delivery service, a garment shop, and the jitney. These constituted "a peripheral if not unimportant feature of the Stelton economy," wrote historian Paul Avrich in his history of the Modern School movement.

It's tempting to see Stelton as a not-quite-suburb—they were anarchists who fled New York when it got too "hot," after all—but that would be a mistake. Stelton is a late example of the mostly nineteenth-century phenomenon of the railroad suburb. Its combination of "ready access to New York with rural privacy and peace," as historian Laurence Veysey put it, was only possible, at that low price, at that historical moment, after the spread of the railroads but before the major waves of suburban development in the 1920s and then after 1945. If Stelton's nonconformist ethos was unusual for a railroad suburb, it was not unique: an earlier parallel is the village of Arden, Delaware, a colony established in 1900 to test economist Henry George's idea of taxing land values as a "single tax." Some residents of Arden commuted by train to Philadelphia. At Stelton, the residential community and the school both depended on the Pennsylvania Railroad. City workers could commute daily; summer and part-time residents could move back and forth with ease; non-resident parents could send their children to school on the train and come to visit without great expense or fuss. In time, private automobiles put jobs in New Brunswick within reach. Meanwhile, Steltonites also contributed to the suburbanization of Middlesex County by building homes and starting their own small businesses.

The decision to relocate to New Jersey—to become suburbanites—had in fact been fraught. Some of the Ferrer leaders worried that away from New York, their political movement would sputter out. Leaving the city seemed like retreat, like acquiescence. But a romantic vision of peasant communes was an important strain in anarchist thought at this time, especially among the Russian Jewish denizens of the Ferrer Center, under the sway of Kropotkin and Tolstoy. Kelly and Abbott later came to believe the move had been a mistake because the movement did peter out and the colonists more or less assimilated to mainstream society. Veysey pointed out that in this respect, they "played the standard life-improvement" game like millions of other new Americans during the twentieth century: "Deliberately leaving aside all questions of intellectual commitment, these colonists might be viewed as immigrant workers who were clever enough to purchase acre plots in the suburbs at a time when land values were still low and few garment workers could hope to escape from the slums." Viewed this way, Stelton gave these families the socioeconomic leg up that many ethnic whites later got in conventional postwar suburbs.

It was more than slow assimilation that ended the dream of an anarchist utopia in the suburbs, however. There were several reasons for Stelton's decline. Anarchism faded as a political philosophy after the Bolsheviks seized power in Russia, and young radicals (including some Steltonites) emigrated to the Soviet Union instead of setting up model communities in the U.S. Although the colony grew during the Depression, the Spanish Civil War divided residents, and the school struggled—and continued to struggle—through World War II. The most drastic change came when the U.S. Army built Camp Kilmer virtually next door, and 75,000 soldiers moved in. Although some struck up friendly relations with the colonists, others had heard rumors about "free love" and wife-swapping and came around to harass women. The school finally closed in 1953 and the remaining colonists trickled away. By the 1970s, it was down to a few holdouts. New development was enfolding and encroaching on the tract.

With a population of Russian and Eastern European Jews, Spaniards, Italians, Brits, and native-born Americans, Stelton was always a diverse place. (In its early days, there were also Native Americans on the school's staff, as well as a Chinese anarchist, Gray Wu.) This diversity had a role in shaping its afterlife. After World War II, the great tide of suburbanization swept into Middlesex County. Black veterans who had been stationed at Camp Kilmer found most suburban areas off-limits to buy houses because of racist practices like redlining and exclusionary covenants. But Steltonites were happy to sell or rent their homes to them. The combination of a growing African-American population and anarchist roots appears to have disturbed the authorities in the 1950s. One former colonist wrote in Scott's book that the FBI visited her several times, "apparently due to the Colony's increasing Black population and the federal fear that radicals would instigate a Black rebellion."

Today, Piscataway has a large black population and an even larger South Asian one. About 45 percent of people in the ZIP code are foreign-born, with a significant number coming from the Indian state of Gujarat. (A Hindu temple sits about 400 feet behind the Goldman House.) It's a fitting echo of the settlers who hailed from Romania and Russia and England and Spain and China, all converging on this piece of New Jersey scrubland in search of "the liberation of the human race through libertarian education"—and, for many, a better quality of life than grim tenements could offer.

The schoolhouse at Stelton burned down in 1955. The library, however, remains. It's now a private home, still tiny but fixed up with new siding and shutters. In the middle of the yard is a plaque framed by tufts of ornamental grass: "Site of The Ferrer Modern School, 1915-1953." Driving around the area today, you can spot many original dwellings—many covered in vinyl siding or sprouting wings on either side, but with the telltale "Stelton shack" at their core. These are peppered among later ranches and split-levels. It's changed from the bucolic homestead that Jon Scott knew, where his father—a self-educated, stubbornly free-thinking farmer—grew potatoes, beets, strawberries, melons, cucumbers, and asparagus. In strawberry season, Scott and his sister would pick the berries, put them in a wheelbarrow, and go down School Street selling them for fifteen cents per quart.

"I think it was the best kind of childhood anybody could ever have," Scott told me. "There was no pressure to be good in school or sports. We were allowed to do things we wanted to do by ourselves. When you do something that you want to do, you're always happy."

———

Stelton certainly didn't strike everyone as paradise. In its first fifteen or twenty years, it looked like a slum to most middle-class eyes, with bare, improvised buildings and unpaved roads strewn with litter. One unimpressed visitor declared, "Such sordid squalor I have never believed possible." Even co-principal Alexis Ferm later said it was "a dump" when he first arrived in 1920. This was the same period when lots in new middle-class suburbs came with exhaustive deed restrictions, stipulating that houses had to sit a certain distance from the street, that residents couldn't take in boarders or keep small farm animals, and that only Caucasians could live there.

The shabby look of the colony bothered some Stelton women enough that they formed a committee, as I learned after stumbling upon a newsletter in the archives at Rutgers. Titled *ACTION*, the newsletter was written and distributed in 1921 by "the Group of Action of Ferrer Colony," which was spearheaded by Esther Shane, Marion Trask, Anna Koch, and Mary Stechbardt. The group called for "prompt action" to counter indifference and self-interest, which, it warned, threatened the colony's aim: "To co-operate in getting away from the petty distrust and exploitation of the city, for the sake of both our children and ourselves." But its main complaint was the colony's appearance. In the "Colony Notes" section, the writer (Mrs. Shane, it seems) praised residents who were doing their part to beautify the neighborhood. The text, possibly a parody of bourgeois home-improvement articles of the time, reads like a cross between Vladimir Lenin and Martha Stewart:

> Failing to secure suitable living quarters or acreage, the Comrades Shane have been offered by Sophie Cohen a quarter acre on which to build. Our secretary will now show us how a Stelton house should look.

> Just see what two cedars, a blue door and yellow curtain can do for a tiny black shack!

> Comrade Tafel has set out some beautiful Norway maples, eight or nine years old, along his driveway. He is also planting some more fruit trees.

Anarchists held divergent views on property ownership. Individualist anarchists endorsed it as a means to live freely, with a measure of protection against the meddling of the state. Those who tilted socialist or Communist might have had qualms, but saw Stelton as a stopgap. In retrospect, it is clear that individual property ownership is what kept Stelton going so long—much longer than most other secular communes. The natural turnover of population and degree of personal investment meant that factionalism, while bitter, could not topple the whole enterprise. (Outside work and the life of the school also helped to counterbalance whatever feuds may have been raging among residents.) Property ownership even saved the colony from destruction during the Red Scare. U.S. Attorney General A. Mitchell Palmer sent federal agents to Stelton. "What saved us," said resident Joseph Cohen, whom they interrogated, "was the fact that we were all property owners, tied up with all kinds of obligations and entanglements." During these years, numerous anarchists were deported from the United States, including Emma Goldman, while Stelton carried on basically untroubled.

What might a Stelton for the twenty-first century look like? Today there is at least one suburban community-around-a-school in the U.S., called Greenbriar, about thirty miles from Austin, Texas. It is an eco-commune on land owned by a nonprofit. For me, Stelton demonstrates the radical possibilities of lowering barriers to homeownership and giving individual homeowners more freedom. Owning a suburban home shouldn't require a high income and big mortgage, as is now the case in many parts of the country. And it shouldn't mean being restricted from taking in boarders or finding other ways to put your land to productive use.

In Stelton, many residents built secondary cottages or shacks on their land to rent out. This has been illegal for decades in the vast majority of American suburbs, and remains so. The

1920s saw the rise of zoning and land-use regulations, which divvied cities and suburbs up into separate commercial, industrial, and residential areas, and imposed a dense layer of rules on what homeowners could do on their own land. One house per lot became the legal limit in most of suburbia (and many urban areas as well). Duplexes, triplexes, and apartments were verboten. Farm animals were banished from many communities.

Now, a shortage of affordable housing pinches many cities and suburbs. There isn't a single county in America where someone can afford a two-bedroom apartment earning the minimum wage. In a number of metropolitan areas on the East and West coasts, it's hard to buy even a modest detached house for less than $500,000. High prices, inflated by scarcity, exclude lower-income people from entire neighborhoods. And because of the country's longstanding racial wealth gap, that burden falls inordinately on people of color.

Thankfully, zoning and land-use regulations are being rethought. New backyard chicken laws in communities around the country have ushered in a return of chickens to urban and suburban land, something that would make sense to the Steltonites who sold their eggs to New Yorkers. More importantly, the state of California, big cities including Washington, D.C., Portland, and Austin, and even a few suburbs (such as Eagan, Minnesota, and Golden, Colorado) have moved to allow backyard cottages and basement apartments, also known as "accessory dwelling units," or ADUs. ADUs accomplish several positive things at once: they increase the supply of housing for small households and people of moderate means; rein in sprawl by accommodating more growth in existing neighborhoods; and give homeowners the option to earn rent to help pay the mortgage or supplement Social Security.

Many ADUs are what are called "tiny houses," dwellings of between 150 and 500 square feet, or about the size of a small apartment. (Of course, Stelton cottages were tiny houses before the term existed: they were rarely larger than a few rooms.)

Thanks to HGTV, tiny houses are an international fad. Those who choose them may be motivated by financial reasons (being locked out of the traditional housing market), the desire to live a more streamlined life, or both. Tiny houses are inherently more climate-friendly than average-sized detached houses, requiring less energy to heat and cool and standing on less land. They are also well-suited to the one- and two-person households prevalent in America today.

The politics around ADUs are tricky. Citizens often oppose them out of concerns over traffic, parking, and increased density. But this "not-in-my-back-yard," or NIMBY, activism faces a growing backlash as the pernicious effects of exclusionary zoning regulations become more widely known. They "don't explicitly discriminate by race, but they effectively exclude families of modest means from entire neighborhoods—and school districts," notes Richard Kahlenberg, an education and housing policy scholar. "These laws promote economic segregation by government fiat."

In late 2018, Senators Cory Booker of New Jersey and Elizabeth Warren of Massachusetts introduced separate bills in Congress to combat exclusionary zoning. Whether one of their bills eventually becomes law or not, their focus on the housing crisis shows that it's becoming hard to ignore as a political issue. A future with backyard cottages—and duplexes and small apartment buildings—dotting hundreds of American cities and suburbs would be a fitting testament to the economic opportunity that Stelton once provided working-class immigrants.

CHAPTER 3

THE RISE AND FALL OF THE NEW DEAL'S GARDEN CITY

Greenbelt, Maryland

Greenbelt was designed so that residents could meet many of their daily needs on foot. It had a movie theater, a cooperative grocery store, an elementary school/community center, and a swimming pool.

The 1939 New York World's Fair, one of the largest ever staged, shrugged off the gloom of the Depression to conjure a bold, bright future—"The World of Tomorrow"—across 1,200 acres in Flushing Meadows, Queens. Forty-four million visitors to the fair toured the giant Futurama exhibit by Norman Bel Geddes and peered at gadgets like an early IBM computer and "Elektro the Moto-Man," a talking robot. Hundreds of thousands of people would have watched a short film screened daily called *The City*. This documentary had been commissioned by the American Institute of Planners and was written by Lewis Mumford, a famous architecture critic and author.

The story the film tells is one of decline: from the attractive small towns and harmonious relations of old America to the towering, anonymous city of steel and concrete. *The City* presents the twentieth-century *homo urbanus* as a cog in a vast, unfeeling machine. In one quick-cut sequence, set to whirling music (by Aaron Copland, who scored the film), customers in a diner slurp their coffee as industrial-sized toasters pop and pancake batter spurts onto a griddle. Hands, mouths, spatulas, and spouts: in the city, they are all parts of the same unfeeling apparatus, the film suggests. In another scene, the music turns ominous as people dodge cars on a busy street where the machines have won out.

But there is a better way. "Science takes flight at last for human goals," the narrator intones over footage of a plane taking off. "This new age builds a better kind of city, close to the soil once more, as molded to our human wants as planes are shaped for speed. ... The new city is organized to make cooperation possible between machines and men and nature." The plane soars over tidy, half-moon villages. "Order has come; order and life together," the voiceover continues. "We've got the skill; we've found the way. We've built the cities. ... We can reproduce the pattern and better it a thousand times."

Boys on bikes whizz past a gleaming-white Modernist building. The path dips below a road and they emerge on the other side, into a park where tall trees shield rows of houses. Welcome to Greenbelt, Maryland, the most potent symbol of the path not taken in suburban development in the United States.

A first-time visitor today might describe Greenbelt as "cute" or "sweet." In its small Art Deco downtown are whitewashed buildings with gracefully rounded corners, housing a movie theater, nail salon, grocery store, and restaurants. Time has whittled its ambitions down to a historical footnote. On a closer look, the place is a bit uncanny, a postcard from a future that failed to materialize.

Once, though, Greenbelt was the "town of tomorrow." When it was still a construction site, on worn-out tobacco fields northeast of Washington, D.C., 350,000 people came to see it. Greenbelt was utterly unlike other new suburbs of the era. Instead of detached houses in the familiar Colonial Revival or bungalow styles, it had rowhouses and apartments that were inspired by progressive European architecture. Instead of a private yard for every family, it had green plazas, footpaths, and underpasses that neighbors shared. Instead of lots and homes priced so that only the well-off could buy them, it was a rental community, with an income ceiling for tenants. It had a beautiful Art Deco school with huge windows and sculptural reliefs, and the rare luxury of a public swimming pool.

Greenbelt was, in a sense, the opposite of Stelton, a radical suburb born not of small-scale improvisation, but deliberate, intense, top-down government action.

The town was a child of the New Deal, specifically of the Resettlement Administration, which President Roosevelt had created with the stroke of a pen to help Americans who were struggling through the Great Depression. Mostly, the RA worked to alleviate the hardships of rural poverty. It built relief camps for migrant workers and subsistence homesteads, where officials hoped that poor farmers, laborers, and coal miners would relocate to grow food and work cooperatively, eventually becoming self-sufficient. (Arthurdale, West Virginia, is the most famous of the homesteads; it was a pet project of First Lady Eleanor Roosevelt.)

But the RA also wanted to fix the run-down, overcrowded neighborhoods where many urban Americans lived. The dire conditions that Jacob Riis chronicled in New York's tenements had improved somewhat since the late nineteenth century, but cities in the 1930s still had large amounts of poor-quality housing. Housing reformers estimated that one-third of Americans were living in "subnormal" conditions—homes that were dark or cramped, or lacked indoor toilets and hot water. (These were mostly rented accommodations; the homeownership rate was well under 50 percent.) To New Deal policy wonks, decentralization was the answer. Build modern, healthful new rental communities on the outskirts of cities, and steer the benighted city-dwellers there.

The RA's administrator was a member of Roosevelt's innermost "brains trust," a debonair, left-wing economist named Rexford Guy Tugwell. In addition to his interest in a planned economy and collectivized agriculture, Tugwell was a firm believer in Ebenezer Howard's Garden City and its potential to alleviate urban overcrowding. "My idea is to go just outside of centers of population, pick up cheap land, build a whole community and entice people into it," Tugwell wrote in his diary in 1935. "I could do this with good heart and he [Roosevelt] now wants me to." Initially, he wanted to build dozens of "greenbelt" towns around the country. That number got whittled down to four: Greendale, Wisconsin, outside of Milwaukee; Greenhills, Ohio, near Cincinnati; Greenbrook, New Jersey (near New Brunswick); and Greenbelt, Maryland.

A government booklet published in 1936 set out the rationale and goals of the program. Under the heading "Is Housing a Public Responsibility?"—a question many readers would have scoffed at—the Resettlement officials answered an unequivocal yes: "If we are to make any real improvement in our housing standards the great bulk of our new housing should be built directly [by the government] for families with modest incomes." On the following pages, a photo spread with the heading "What Other Nations Are Doing" featured attractive public-housing projects in Belgium, Switzerland, Germany, Britain, and Sweden.

The RA's foray into town-building was relatively modest. The new communities would have no more than 1,500 houses each. But Tugwell hoped they would spark an urban-planning revolution. "Every growing metropolis should—if it is wisely planned—develop a chain of similar suburban communities around its borders," Tugwell, or one of his deputies, declared in the RA booklet. Their vision was hundreds of government-owned, mixed-use suburban towns, inhabited by ordinary families, from sea to shining sea.

―――――――――

For months, George Warner, a low-level employee of the U.S. State Department who lived in Bethesda, Maryland, had been reading about Greenbelt in the papers on his commute. He knew it was a demonstration town, built by the federal government for families of modest means, like his own. He knew that businesses in the town would be organized as cooperatives, with any profits returning to residents. The more he read about it, the more excited he got.

George and his wife, Claire, put their names on the list of prospective tenants. Federal tenant-selection officers interviewed them about their motives for moving, their personal interests, and what they hoped to contribute to the new community. With more than 5,700 families vying for 885 homes, the Warners' odds were slim. But at the end of 1937, an envelope marked "Resettlement Division, Farm Security Administration" arrived in their mailbox. They were in.

George, Claire, and their two children spent the next several evenings deep in discussion, as Warner recounted in his memoir:

> We realized that there would be many drawbacks. We would be leaving home and friends to take up residence in a new town among new people. We would spent much of our time commuting between Greenbelt and Washington. We would be engaging in an untried experiment which gave no assurance of success. We would be letting the whole world know that we were a so-called low-income family.

> On the other hand, we would be getting a fresh start under the best possible auspices. We would have the satisfaction of exercising such talents as we possessed in a community dedicated to progress. ... We would become part of a classless society composed of persons of our own income status, where worth would be measured in terms of contribution to community welfare. We could grow in a soil dedicated to democratic citizenship and derive those satisfactions which stem from working with others toward a common goal.

The Warners chose a corner row house on Greenbelt's Ridge Road. It had a living room, a dining room, a modern electric kitchen, a bathroom with a constant supply of hot water, and three bedrooms—luxurious accommodations at a time when many families crammed into two or three rooms due to a severe housing shortage. When the family moved into their new home in Spring 1938, they found it "all that we could desire ... designed for healthful, convenient, and congenial living."

Their unit was one of some 500 row homes built in Greenbelt's first phase. These were constructed both out of wood, with brick veneers and pitched roofs, in an updated English-cottage style, and out of concrete block with flat roofs, in a restrained Bauhaus mode. Hedges, not fences, separated yards. Houses were wider than they were deep, with long horizontal axes that admitted copious light and encouraged ventilation. For all their outward simplicity, the houses had ten different floor plans. The twelve apartment buildings built at the same time are more bluntly Modernist than the row houses, with white concrete-block walls and three-story panels of glass block on their main facades. A few detached prefab houses were also built to test new construction methods.

Whether apartment building or house-row, the residential structures at Greenbelt all have a "service side" and a "garden side": The typical orientation of a house to the street is flipped. That is, the entrance accessible by car is the "back," for services like trash, laundry, and parking, while the entrance at the rear of the house is the "front," giving onto parkland and pedestrian footpaths. The "garden side"/"service side" concept was pioneered by architects Clarence Stein and Henry Wright in Radburn, New Jersey, in the late 1920s.

You can get a better sense of the Warners' home life on a visit to the Greenbelt Museum, which occupies one of the original attached houses on Crescent Road. A flat-roofed, concrete-block model, the house is presented almost exactly as it might have appeared in 1937, with period furniture and the shiny black flooring that designers chose for how it hid dirt. Casement windows open out for ventilation. The kitchen is small but laid out for hygiene and efficiency, with copious drawers and cabinets, a refrigerator, a double sink, and sockets for electrical appliances. When the *Washington Post*'s food editor visited Greenbelt, she found the homes' kitchens to be "trail blazers along lines of convenience and labor saving." On the service side of the house, facing the road, a clothesline hangs between posts and is partly masked by hedges. The small porch on this side cleverly conceals a closet for rakes and gardening equipment, and a metal circle in the ground next to the porch is the inconspicuous lid of a buried garbage receptacle. On the court side, the house looks onto a green common with trees, a playground, and criss-crossing paths.

When Roosevelt created the RA and named Tugwell its administrator, he gave him $31 million for building the greenbelt towns—a small slice of the $4.9 billion Emergency Relief Appropriation Act. (The rest went to programs including rural electrification and the Works Progress Administration.) Roosevelt's allocation came with a catch: Tugwell would have to use WPA teams of mostly unskilled transient workers to build the towns. Before any blueprints were ready, the WPA sent men to the Greenbelt site; they were hurriedly instructed to start digging the town's lake. (Which they did with picks and shovels—the use of heavy machinery was avoided, since a main goal of the project was to put men to work.) The planners could hardly finish drawings fast enough.

Despite the time pressure, these planners and architects, working under Hale Walker and culled from among the country's brightest young talent, worked thoughtfully. They curved the town into a gentle horseshoe to take advantage of a natural plateau, and oriented it to catch prevailing breezes. Houses were designed so that low-skilled laborers would be able to build them, and durable materials were specified to reduce maintenance costs. They even had customized furniture, thanks to designers in the Special Skills Division of the RA. The sturdy wooden pieces were streamlined to fit the small units, and designed for versatility: phone tables could also be nightstands; tables could extend as a family grew. Residents were able to buy the furniture on an installment plan. "On August 1, 1939, Claire and I purchased some pieces of furniture from our government," wrote Warner, clearly enjoying the implausibility of the transaction.

By the time the town was fully settled by families like the Warners—none earning more than about $2,000 a year ($35,000 in today's money)—it had a population of 3,000. Children scampered down the paths and through a specially built pedestrian underpass to get to the elementary school, run by the federal government with a progressive curriculum. After hours, the school served as a community center, a double role conceived not just for efficiency's sake but, architect Douglas Ellington said, because it "made possible greater social unity" in the town, blending educational and civic life.

The town's early residents were young, energetic, and believed they were ushering in a more egalitarian future. As one original Greenbelter recalled years later, "It was really like a frontier community where you didn't bring in your ancestry and your D.A.R. [Daughters of the American Revolution] connections. You contributed and you were taken for what you were, at face value." Another, echoing Warner's remark about a classless society, wrote: "There was no hierarchy here, no rich people looking down on the peasants. We were all equal."

In the 1920s, the growth rate of the suburbs had overtaken that of central cities, yet houses in the suburbs remained expensive and mortgage terms were difficult (mortgages typically had to be paid back within seven years). Less than half of Americans owned their homes. Herbert Hoover, first as commerce secretary and then as president, saw increasing the homeownership rate as crucial for producing independent citizens and a healthy economy. Hoover launched campaigns to stimulate private homebuilding, and soon, developers began to build large residential suburbs outside of American cities. Yet the homeownership rate ticked up only a bit, to 48 percent, and dropped again when the Depression struck. Now, Hoover's successor had built a carefully planned suburban community for the American majority—renters. It offered modern housing, plenty of greenery and fresh air, and almost everything a family could desire within a five-minute walk. (Almost: transportation to Washington remained a stubborn problem, after an early commuter bus service proved unviable.)

The strong emphasis on co-ops and cooperation in general by Greenbelt's planners reflects a characteristically 1930s striving for a "middle way" between plutocratic capitalism and state socialism at a time when liberal democracy was under threat. Residents took it to heart. Some may have even believed that the "Greenbelt spirit" could defend the American way of life. One Greenbelter suggested as much in a letter to the *Washington Evening Star*, published months before the outbreak of World War II:

> We in Greenbelt have learned that, though as individuals we are feeble, as a group we have power. We have learned the significance and potentiality of united social action—and what greater lesson must our people learn if our democracy is to survive?

President Roosevelt toured the half-built Greenbelt in 1936. He spent two hours at the site, asking questions about various projects and watching as the first fish were thrown into the lake. Afterward, he told reporters, "[Greenbelt] is an experiment that ought to be copied by every community in the United States."

This should have been a triumph for Rex Tugwell, who accompanied the president on his tour. But four days later, he resigned as head of the RA. Tugwell had become a political liability for Roosevelt. In his previous role as assistant secretary of agriculture, he'd drawn the ire of both the drug and publishing industries when he tried to stop false advertising of patent (or "quack") medicines. Opponents accused "Rex the Red" of harboring communist sympathies, noting that he visited the Soviet Union in 1927 (he had gone with a trade delegation to study Soviet agriculture). In 1934, an Indiana school superintendent named William Wirt testified before a Congressional committee that he had learned the New Deal was really a plot led by Tugwell, the "Stalin" figure who would eventually oust "Kerensky" (Roosevelt) and overthrow the American government. Tugwell's academic air and movie-star looks fueled further criticism. Journalists cast him as an ivory-tower dreamer out of touch with the real world, "the man with no dirt on his shoes."

Given the cloud of controversy around Tugwell, his suburban scheme received a drubbing in the press. A *Washington Post* columnist wrote, "Like all things Tugwellian, it is far different from accepted ideas—at least, far from those accepted in America." The *Chicago American* newspaper announced that the "first communist towns in America" were coming to fruition. Greenbelt—located on Washington's doorstep, with a throng of journalists nearby—drew most of the scrutiny, and criticism. The *Post* nicknamed it "Tugwell's Folly" and "Tugwelltown" and characterized it as a boondoggle. There was some truth to that, although the intention was never for Greenbelt to demonstrate cost-effectiveness in construction; it was meant to put a lot of men to work.

The newspapers softened once Tugwell was gone and the town was up and running (many Greenbelters were now subscribers, after all). By late 1937, the *Post's* editorial page admitted, "The model communities built by RA, such as the one at Berwyn, with which Washingtonians are most familiar, have a tangible value as well as a potential social value that should not be minimized, however uneconomically they were constructed." In 1941, after passage of the Lanham Act, the government hastily built 1,000 new homes for defense workers on a site north of Greenbelt's first phase. But a radical reputation stuck to Greenbelt. Visitors still came to gawk at the inhabitants and detect signs of social engineering.

Greenbelt's image as a place apart persisted until at least the 1950s, when a resident named Abraham Chasanow was suspended from his U.S. Navy job as a security risk. An unnamed informant had charged him with being "a leader and very active in a radical group in Greenbelt, Md.," and an associate of "people who had Communistic tendencies." Chasanow was eventually exonerated, and the case was made into a Hollywood movie, *Three Brave Men*. Living in Greenbelt seems to have made Chasanow appear more suspicious to authorities, although anti-Semitism probably also played a role in his treatment.

Ironically, Chasanow was a Republican voter and about as rule-following as they came, head of the local Lions Club and PTA. Greenbelt was more radical in its form and implied social contract than in its residents' political opinions. Greenbelters did lean to the left, but there was a spectrum; 58 percent identified as Democrats, 34 percent as independents, and 13 percent as Republicans. Although co-ops flourished in the town at midcentury, so did the more conventional American Legion post, which grew to become the largest in the state of Maryland.

There were two major social aspects in which Greenbelt was not only less than radical, but reactionary. First, when the town opened, women were not allowed to work. This was presumably to ensure that households did not exceed the income limit, but it had the effect of keeping women at home (until the war years, when the government changed the policy). Although the town provided apartments for single men and couples in accordance with their share of the population, the nuclear family with a stay-at-home mother was almost as normative in Greenbelt as it would late be in privately built suburbs. As in those suburbs, women in Greenbelt could feel quite isolated.

Second, and much worse, African Americans were barred from living in Greenbelt, despite having worked on the crews that built it. Originally, there was going to be a separate development for black families on the Greenbelt site, but "[o]fficials quietly dropped the plan," according to a history of the town by Cathy Knepper. It may be true that, as Knepper wrote, "in 1937 America a racially integrated community would have been not only an anomaly but totally unacceptable to the citizens of Prince George's County." But the decision to exclude blacks from Greenbelt exemplifies how the New Deal entrenched racism even as it furthered progressive aims like building the welfare state. While Tugwell's RA tinkered with progressive planning off on the sidelines, the federal Home Owners' Loan Corporation (or HOLC) was drawing up maps that financially redlined many black urban neighborhoods around the country, ruling them dangerous for lending. That greatly exacerbated racial segregation and led to a long-term decline in home ownership and home values in inner-city neighborhoods. The underwriting manual of the New Deal-era Federal Housing Administration housing also codified racism, warning that "incompatible racial groups should not be permitted to live in the same communities"—a rule that Greenbelt's creators didn't flout.

Even a plan as bold in many ways as Tugwell's mounted absolutely no challenge to white supremacy. Megan Searing Young, the director of the Greenbelt Museum, told me a big part of her mission is underscoring that fact for students and visitors. "We still need to talk about [how] it's this utopian experiment—utopia if you were a white family," she said.

Lewis Mumford believed that Greenbelt and the other RA towns had set a pattern that would define a new age. He was wrong. The fourth town planned by the RA, Greenbrook, New Jersey, never materialized, let alone dozens more. Greenbrook provoked a legal challenge by disgruntled landowners. In *Franklin Township v. Tugwell* (1936), the U.S. Court of Appeals in the District of Columbia ruled that the law appropriating funds for the RA was unconstitutional. A few years later, the country entered World War II, and after victory was declared in 1945, the private construction industry roared into action (with a big assist from the federal government) to supply homes for returning veterans. It, not Greenbelt, set the mold for twentieth-century suburbia.

The subsequent history of Greenbelt reveals the problem with designing to ameliorate social and economic conditions: those conditions always change. In the 1930s, a well-designed, three-bedroom townhouse was more than adequate for a lower-middle-class family. Garden courts were the perfect gathering place for young children, who made up half of Greenbelt's population. "You didn't just sit in your house and your little nuclear family and eat your dinner and all that," said Sheila Maffay-Tuthill, a third-generation town resident who is the education and volunteer coordinator at the Greenbelt Museum. "A lot of the social construct was based around your court. Everybody in a court became so, so close. It was like family."

Now, higher standards of living and ballooning home sizes have made 800 square feet seem stingy. And in retrospect, the garden side/service side plan underestimated the social effects of mass car ownership, while the emphasis on courts presumed a captive audience of women and children. Cars allowed Americans to expand their range of activity, and more married women began to work outside the home and have fewer children. Today, Greenbelt's courts are sleepy except for the odd dog walker or parent and toddler. Some homes appear to have reverted to a regular front-and-back orientation.

Nevertheless, in many ways, Greenbelt is still worth emulating seventy-five years after its unlikely birth. The Thirties core is walkable, with the library and shopping center a short stroll away from housing blocks. The original homes may not suffice for many families of five, but they're attractive to smaller households and can be purchased for about $200,000—a bargain in the pricey Washington area, even after adding on several hundred dollars a month in co-op fees. Historic Greenbelt is still home to some families with young children, but it is more popular with older people, especially retirees. "A lot of people have chosen to age in place here. They call it a NORC—'Naturally Occurring Retirement Community,'" Maffay-Tuthill told me. "Because as you're living your years here in the co-operative homes, you're getting all the maintenance done for you. It's very walkable, so a lot of people look at it and say, 'Why would I move from here? With a few adaptations, it's a really great place to be a retiree and live out the rest of my life.'"

I heard something similar from Isabelle Gournay, an architecture professor at the University of Maryland who has lived in Greenbelt for fifteen years. Over a dinner of squash and leek crepes at the New Deal Café, a venerable and much-loved co-op, Gournay told me about life in an "implemented utopia," as she calls it. Raised in Paris, she prizes being able to walk to shops, the swimming pool, and the movies, but she also appreciates Greenbelt's small-town friendliness. "It's really nice to go to the supermarket and, every time, meet someone you know," she said. "Living in Paris, my dad, he hardly knows anyone. It's not so congenial. And because I have a degree in architecture, I do feel the planning principles in action here. The pathways. The underpasses. The sequence of playgrounds—it's very scenic. The houses may be standardized, but [the plan] really creates a sense of intimacy with nature."

Although it was the creation of Uncle Sam, Greenbelt was not a federal fiefdom for long. The town was incorporated and a local government established on the council-manager model. After the New Deal era, Greenbelt lacked visionary planning guidance, and it sprawled into the usual, desultory subdivisions and garden apartments. First the Baltimore-Washington Parkway and then the Capital Beltway sliced through the town, creating barriers that have proved hard to overcome. In Historic Greenbelt (east of the Beltway), the effects of the racist tenant-selection process are still perceptible—it is whiter than the neighborhoods surrounding it. But this has been countered by the larger trend of African Americans settling throughout Prince George's County, making it the most affluent majority-black county in the nation, and by waves of immigrant arrivals. Non-Hispanic whites are now a minority in the 24,000-person City of Greenbelt. The city's population is now 51 percent black and 15 percent Hispanic or Latino. Two members of the seven-person city council are black; the first was elected in 2009, after the city added council seats in response to a complaint from the NAACP and ACLU that Greenbelt's at-large voting system was disenfranchising minority voters. If Historic Greenbelt represents an idealized suburban past, the suburb of the present is on display at Beltway Plaza Mall in West Greenbelt, where the shoppers are predominantly Central American and African and the food court serves jollof rice and *lengua* tacos.

Increasingly, architects, planners, public officials, and ordinary citizens are noticing a gap in American neighborhoods that places like Greenbelt once filled. Where are the houses that are smaller and closer together than a tract of single-family homes, but not as dense as apartments downtown? This has become known as the "missing middle." The category includes housing types that used to be common: townhouses and smaller apartment buildings like those at Greenbelt, but also duplexes, triplexes, and regional variations like the bungalow courts of California. Architect Daniel Parolek, who coined the term "missing middle," has called it "affordable by design" because smaller units usually sell or rent for less. It's a major problem that Greenbelt-style housing is impossible to build in most suburban areas in America, especially given the housing cost burden that so many people now bear. At the time of this writing, Minneapolis has just voted to rezone all residential neighborhoods in the city for up to three-unit properties (triplexes). Hopefully, this reform will ripple out to suburban jurisdictions soon.

Greenbelt also anticipated the current surge in mixed-use development. Historic Greenbelt's downtown may look trifling, but it meets most of the daily needs of residents like Gournay. Now that the city has grown so much, the Art Deco school building (repurposed as a community center) and swimming pool don't seem like over-the-top expenditures: they seem far-sighted. Building them to such a high standard was an act of generosity and optimism that's humbling in an age when even basic public services must justify their existence.

Early Greenbelters were all white, shared a general sympathy for (or at least were not antagonistic to) the New Deal project, and made similar amounts of money. But in their politics and religious beliefs, they could be quite different. (Conscientious objectors and veterans argued bitterly, for instance, and there was friction between residents of "Old Greenbelt" and the defense homes.) What people opted into by moving to Greenbelt did not require a high level of dedication or self-abnegation. Yet a shared identity took root, and endured.

"They called themselves 'pioneers in a new way of living,'" Young said of Greenbelt's first residents. We were sitting in the house next to the museum, which it has purchased and plans to expand into. "We might, with jaded twenty-first-century eyes, see it as kind of goofy," she continued. "But they really were engaged in that. A lot of that emphasis on citizen activism has transmitted through the years, and somewhat because there are families that have lived here that long. But I think it's also because of the way the community operates. Many of the people who live here really do believe that co-operatives are a viable alternative to capitalism." Greenbelt still has at least seven co-ops, including the housing co-op, a grocery store, a nursery school, a credit union, and the weekly paper, the *News Review* (formerly the *Cooperator*), which hasn't missed an issue since 1937.

After World War II, at least one high-ranking federal official hoped not only to maintain the greenbelt towns as government demonstration projects, but to extend them to their original planned size. But the tide was turning against collectivist programs. In 1949, President Truman signed a law that allowed the government to divest itself of the towns. Greenbelters formed a housing co-op and bought 1,600 homes and several hundred acres of open land, with the intention of building more housing in keeping with the Garden City plan. But when taxes on the undeveloped land mounted, the co-op sold it, losing a chance to oversee the sympathetic development of new neighborhoods.

A true Garden City in Maryland never came to pass. The vision shared by Tugwell, Mumford, and Stein went against the American grain of individualism—but more to the point, it enraged powerful industries. By the late Forties, "A conservative alliance of building, real estate, banking, and chamber of commerce organizations ... adamantly opposed providing funds for public housing as a 'socialistic' intrusion into the private market," according to Alexander von Hoffman. While Greenbelt passed out of federal hands, the vision of dignified, egalitarian public housing withered. Truman's Housing Act of 1949 established limited funds for local governments to build public housing but, under pressure from the business lobby, restricted it to the very poor, with low ceilings on tenants' incomes as well as rents (so as not to compete with the private market). In the years that followed, cities often relegated public housing to inferior sites, and suburbs resisted building it at all. Greenbelt towns aside, the U.S. did not build social housing on the urban periphery as many European countries did. The Garden City model gave way to the *Ville Radieuse*, Le Corbusier's functionalist utopia of megalithic towers in a park. Soon, high-rise public-housing became associated with broken elevators and crime-ridden "streets in the sky." In the late 1950s, Catherine Bauer, a leading public-housing advocate who helped draft FDR's Housing Act of 1937, looked back with disappointment on where it all went wrong:

> While everybody who had any choice was moving into a one-story home, the housing authorities were busily erecting high-density high-rise apartments, with no private outdoor space whatever. Significantly, perhaps, public housing is most accepted in the one American city where apartment living is also most taken for granted—New York. But even there, opinion surveys show that most tenants would prefer ground-level living if they could get it.

Greenbelt's moderate income range was born out of expediency—Congressional budget cuts had made renting to the truly low-income unviable. But if the friendly scale of Greenbelt housing and its higher income cap had become programmatic, American public housing might have attracted more support, and maybe today, "[t]he idea of public housing would be taken for granted, like old age pensions or FHA mortgage insurance," in Bauer's words.

Recently, housing advocates on the left have argued for a national program of public-housing construction to ease the affordability crisis. Given the long bias against public housing, that seems unlikely to happen any time soon. Existing public housing is chronically underfunded, and the main mechanism of funding affordable housing in the U.S., the Low-Income Housing Tax Credit, is politically vulnerable. Although they can only ever be partial solutions, limited-equity cooperatives (like Greenbelt Homes), community land trusts, and mutual housing associations curb speculation and ensure long-term affordability for renters and owners alike. There's also what's known as inclusionary zoning: Montgomery County, Maryland, where I live, requires that developers reserve a percentage of new units as "moderately priced dwelling units"; these have sales-price and rent caps, and can only be sold or rented to people making less than the area median income.

Ironically, Greenbelt did presage one kind of community that many suburbanites live in now: the private master-planned community. Often, such developments have large single-family homes sprinkled around a golf course, with no (or very few) commercial enterprises. But a more holistic master-planned community with some parallels to Greenbelt exists in South Jordan, Utah, outside of Salt Lake City. Laid out by the New Urbanist architect and planner Peter Calthorpe, Daybreak has detached houses in contemporary and traditional styles as well as missing-middle townhouses, cottage clusters, and small condo buildings. There's also a downtown with offices and stores, parkland and wetlands, and light-rail service to Salt Lake City. Most children in Daybreak walk to school, which is now an anomaly (only 20 percent of schoolchildren walk nationwide).

Since Daybreak is a private development, its 20,000 residents are required to join and follow the rules of the Daybreak Community Association. Daybreak even has *sub*-HOAs and condo associations under the aegis of the larger HOA, and some residents pay dues to both. HOAs and condo associations can actually be traced back to the New Deal era. As political scientist Evan McKenzie explains in his book *Privatopia*, the nonprofit quasi-government set up for Radburn, New Jersey—Greenbelt's predecessor—became a national prototype. Developers found it an extremely convenient way to hand off management responsibilities and assuage buyers that their investment in the neighborhood would be safe from deterioration.

But what binds residents of these communities together is not cooperation for the greater good, as at Greenbelt, but the maintenance of property values. They are also less than democratic: renters are disenfranchised, since usually only homeowners can vote, and the only way to change an HOA or condominium rule is often with a "super-majority" vote of 75 percent of all members. Because of this, McKenzie considers HOAs and condos perversions of Ebenezer Howard's ideals. Howard's hope for "'a new civilisation based on service to the community and not on self-interest' has not been realized," McKenzie writes. "Instead, American real estate development corporations, with government as a silent partner, have chosen to build a new kind of community that serves as a monument to privatism."

When Rex Tugwell's dream of suburb-building in the public interest died, attempts to bring Modernist design and a spirit of cooperation to suburbia lost some momentum. But they did not stop. Over the next few decades, idealistic builders and architects around the country made their peace with privatism, yet tried to bend it to progressive aims.

CHAPTER 4

WHEN THE BAUHAUS MET THE SUBDIVISION

Six Moon Hill and Five Fields,
Lexington, Massachusetts

At Five Fields, built on a former dairy farm, houses' setbacks were staggered and their orientations varied according to the gentle rises and falls of the land.

Members of The Architects Collaborative, left to right: Sarah (Sally) Harkness, Jean B. Fletcher, Robert S. McMillan, Norman C. Fletcher, Walter Gropius, John C. (Chip) Harkness, Benjamin Thompson, and Louis A. McMillen.

In March 1947, the *Boston Globe* profiled an unusual *ménage* on its woman's page, in an article about the domestic arrangements of two women architects with young children. "For more than a year," the writer recounted primly but with evident admiration, "brunette Jean Fletcher and blonde Sally Harkness have shared a house, a maid and baby sitters. And both of them have jobs with the Architects' Collaborative in Harvard [Square], where their husbands, Norman and John, also work."

The article explained how the Fletcher and Harkness families, with four children between them, divvied up a single Cambridge residence. The Harknesses got the ground floor and the yard; the Fletchers, the top two floors. Everyone shared a washing machine and telephone. Sally Harkness and Jean Fletcher worked staggered half-days at the office so that they could split the wages of a maid, who watched the children while they worked and did some of the household chores.

Friends for several years, the couples had renovated the house to give each family more privacy and to reflect their Modernist tastes.

(The *Globe* noted then-bohemian interior touches like plain stools and walls painted bright colors.) Sally Harkness told the paper that the semi-shared household was healthy for the children, because of the yard and other open spaces nearby, and convenient for the adults.

However, it was not her first choice. "[T]he ideal way," she said, "would be with the building of new single units in a small neighborhood. This could develop eventually into a large community, with shops, schools and sitters available for all."

Maybe Harkness was prophetic. But more likely, she was already planning such a neighborhood, giving it definite contours in her mind's eye. Sometime during the winter of 1946-7, a few of the twenty-something architects had gone cross-country skiing west of Cambridge, in the countryside around Lexington. They'd traversed a hill with oak and pine trees, noting both its privacy and its easy access to Cambridge and Boston. In May 1947—a couple of months after the *Globe* article appeared—the Fletchers and Harknesses, along with their colleagues in The Architects' Collaborative, or TAC, bought the 20-acre site. They called the new neighborhood Six Moon Hill, after the old Moon-brand cars that had been left in a barn on the property.

The war was hardly behind them. Ben Thompson, another TAC member, had served in the Navy for four years. John ("Chip") Harkness had registered as a conscientious objector, then driven ambulances for the American Field Service during battles in Italy. Now, their hope was to build a community that not only allowed them to live in peace, but actively fostered it.

"The desire to develop a community 'of more than routine interest' was present in everyone's mind," Norman "Fletch" Fletcher wrote almost two decades later of TAC at this time. "[A]lso the conviction that cooperative principles were important. There was, and is, a strong conviction at TAC that ideal communities go far toward preventing social conflict."

TAC was composed of Walter Gropius, the legendary founder of the Bauhaus, and several of his protégés. Through Gropius, the younger architects imbibed the ethos of designing collaboratively across disciplines—gathering architecture, urban planning, landscape architecture, and industrial design into their purview. And they upheld the Bauhaus tenet that design ought to be a force for a better, more egalitarian society.

Gropius, steeped in Garden City thinking himself, had led design studios at Harvard that cast America's housing shortage as a "town building problem" and encouraged students to imagine new suburban "townships" on the highways to Boston. The philosophies of Ebenezer Howard, the Bauhaus, and the New Deal (with its recent high-profile experiment of Greenbelt) commingled in the minds of young designers. But with the New Deal and the war now both over, so was the government-directed command urbanism that produced Greenbelt. A new suburban paradigm was emerging, of private firms buying up vast tracts of peripheral land and putting hundreds or thousands of houses on it, using techniques of mass production to build them very fast and at low cost. As TAC began to design innovative Modernist houses in the Boston suburb of Lexington, some 200 miles down the Eastern seaboard, Levitt & Sons was building the first phase of Levittown, New York, which grew to a staggering 17,500 houses by 1951.

One reason for the Levitts' success was their adherence to the conservative design guidelines of the Federal Housing Administration, which insured a large share of home mortgages. The FHA, concerned about resale value, warned builders off Modernist and experimental design and advocated the use of "safe" styles like Cape Cod and Colonial Revival. The FHA also advised that developments should be racially homogeneous. In the agency's eyes, the larger and more monotonous a tract of housing, the better, because the lower the risk to "neighborhood stability."

It's obvious which model won out. But in TAC's quest to create a superior suburb for the everyman, we get a tantalizing look at a different trajectory for the postwar suburbs, one that emphasized progressive architecture, a blurring of private and public space, and semi-wild nature. Unlike Greenbelt's planners, TAC's architects did not challenge the suburban pattern of residential enclaves of detached homes. Instead, they tried to optimize it for families with children. The enduring cachet of TAC's two developments in Lexington testifies to their success, and to the real, mostly unmet demand for nontraditional design in suburbia today.

———

All of the younger architects in TAC built houses for their own families on the hill. (Gropius stayed in the house he'd built in 1938 in Lincoln, nine miles to the west, now a National Historic Landmark.) They subdivided the land into twenty-nine half-acre lots, plus common area and an access road. The other lots were claimed by friends and associates, as well as young professionals who had heard about the novel community going up in Lexington. To pick their home sites, the first twelve couples drew numbers out of a hat, this being seen as most equitable. The "Collaborative" in the firm's name was deliberate—the designers had envisioned a non-hierarchical practice of equals working together, a break with the typical architecture office of the time (and of our time), in which one feted architect or a few partners preside over a corps of overworked, overlooked junior employees. Accordingly, TAC wanted Six Moon Hill to be a co-op, but this wasn't possible under Massachusetts law. Instead, they formed a corporation, Six Moon Hill, Inc., that owned and maintained the common land. Each household received two shares, so spouses could vote differently if they chose to. Those who bought in had to secure private mortgages, since the FHA would not insure houses built in such a modern style.

The overall architectural effect that TAC sought was variety in unity, not strict uniformity. Although the houses shared a common vocabulary of flat or shed roofs, vertical redwood or cypress cladding, large windows, and strong horizontal lines, their floor plans varied considerably, with some venturing further into experimental territory than others—especially in the architects' own residences. TAC's Bob MacMillan, for example, put the bedrooms of his house in a half-basement and treated the ground floor as a continuous live-work space, with a glass wall on the south side to take advantage of a good view. Leonard Currie, an architect who worked with TAC but was not a member of the partnership, hung a wooden ramp from his house by cables to give direct access to the kitchen while preserving the natural slope of the ground. The Harknesses, wishing to extend their kitchen-dining area-playroom to the outdoors in nice weather, braced large windows with steel ties and attached hardware so the windows could be raised overhead, like garage doors. They also used domed Plexiglas skylights to brighten the playroom. At the time, TAC was working with the manufacturer of Plexiglas, Rohm & Haas, to find peacetime applications for the material, which had been used in bomber-plane noses and turrets during the war.

Perhaps most unusual home on the hill was that of TAC's Louis McMillen (no relation to his colleague Bob McMillan). This was composed of two rectangular volumes placed at different elevations on a steep site, and connected by a narrow, stepped, glass-walled link. One wing held a living/dining area, kitchen, and basement playroom; the other contained three bedrooms and a bathroom. The McMillen House had Plexiglas skylights and a fireplace covered by a parabolic hood of white concrete.

Of course, architects have long designed custom homes with novel, eye-catching features, and still do today. The difference at Six Moon Hill is that TAC's clients (including the designers themselves) were not wealthy executives with live-in help. They were mostly in their late twenties and early thirties, and just embarking on careers after the war, with babies in tow or on the way. Moon Hill houses ranged in price from $10,000 to $22,000. That was certainly a rung or two above Levittown, where the first houses sold for about $7,000, but at the lower end, it was within the budget of many families living on one junior academic or professional salary. (Adjusted for inflation, $10,000 in 1950 is about $105,000 today.)

Keeping costs down was therefore a necessity. TAC abandoned its initial idea to loop Moon Hill Road around the outside of the parcel and leave the middle as a pedestrian way (in Greenbelt fashion), because this would have been too expensive. It opted instead for a shorter and therefore cheaper cul-de-sac road between the home sites. Despite all the custom touches in the houses, their footprints were as compact as 1,100 square feet. Customizations were made for efficiency as well as for aesthetic reasons. One house had an oak table that rested on tracks between the kitchen and dining room. Pushed one way, it was a dining table; pushed the other, it was a counter. The architects also subtly pushed back against the gendered logic of residential design of the era. Instead of being fully enclosed, their kitchens often had pass-throughs to the dining or living area with open shelves above, ensuring that whoever was in the kitchen (usually the woman of the house) would not be cut off from what was happening in other rooms. Playrooms were often put in the basement; TAC seems to have assumed that the mothers of Six Moon Hill would not want to hover over their children.

Bedrooms were small, even by the standards of the day. This was a space-saving measure, but not just that, said Sandra Galejs and Peter Warren, current Moon Hill residents who got to know Sally Harkness before her death at age ninety-eight in 2013. Harkness and her colleagues purposely designed large living areas and smaller bedrooms "to propel people out of the bedrooms and to join each other in the common areas," Warren recalled Sally Harkness telling her. The designers' vision of Moon Hill as a modern village, not a collection of atomized private houses, shaped the dimensions of the rooms themselves. It also resulted in a no-fences rule. (To this day, there are no fences between the houses.)

In 1954, *Vogue* ran an effusive profile of the neighborhood titled "The Good Life, Inc." Next to a full-page photograph of couples smoking and talking in a double-height living room, a woman in a stylish Jens Risom chair with her back to the camera, the article noted that "these families have an almost pioneer attitude of mutual help, friendliness, and purpose ... doors aren't locked and everyone calls everyone by his given name and the first person met in any one house is apt to be someone else's child."

The sense of camaraderie was strong. "We kids all had LOTS of parents," wrote one man who grew up on Moon Hill in a memory book published for its fiftieth anniversary in 1997. "Most parents were called by their first names ... I can honestly say that I knew the first names of all but maybe ten of the people living on the road." The memory book is full of stories of kids camping and building forts in the woods and hunting for Easter eggs on the abandoned golf course nearby (which was later developed). In 1960, the association built a pool on the common land, and it became the social hub in summer months. In the winter, kids went sledding down the hill while their parents climbed ladders to remove the snow from their roofs, calling across to each other as they shoveled.

The late 1940s and 1950s saw the mushrooming of large-tract, assembly-line-built suburbs like the Levittowns, Park Forest, Illinois, and Lakewood, California. Meanwhile, a number of Modernist subdivisions cropped up outside of U.S. cities. In northern Virginia, close to Washington, D.C., architect Charles

Goodman and landscape architect Dan Kiley designed Hollin Hills, 450 homes tucked in rolling woodland. In California, a builder named Joseph Eichler developed tracts of homes designed by Modernist architects. The phrase "Eichler Home" is now synonymous with post-and-beam construction, cathedral ceilings, atriums and patios, and glass walls. (Unlike TAC's communities, Eichler's had private yards.) In the Midwest, George Fred Keck—who designed the "House of Tomorrow" for the 1933 Chicago World's Fair—built a subdivision of early solar houses in Glencoe, Illinois, with his brother William. In Colorado, businessman Edward Hawkins collaborated with architect Eugene Sternberg on Arapahoe Acres near Denver.

Even the master himself, Frank Lloyd Wright, got in on the act. In 1945, a group of his disciples convinced Wright to help them build a cooperative community on a tract near Pleasantville in Westchester County. Wright designed three houses and approved the plans for forty-odd more by other architects. The neighborhood was called Usonia, and it drew on the vision behind Wright's "Usonian" homes—compact, unpretentious homes designed for the everyman. (Wright also designed one-off Usonians, some of them in suburban locations, like the Pope-Leighey House in northern Virginia, not far from Hollin Hills.)

But nowhere saw as much of this activity as the western arc of Boston's suburbs, and especially Lexington. The site of the first battle of the Revolutionary War, the "birthplace of American liberty" was a hybrid of farming community and streetcar suburb until the rumblings of major suburbanization after World War II. Just fifteen minutes northwest of Cambridge on the recently upgraded Route 2, Lexington was conveniently located for academics at Harvard and MIT. In 1951, Lincoln Laboratory, a federally funded MIT lab for radar research, and companies like Raytheon arrived along Route 128, increasing the town's appeal to scientists and engineers. From 1940 to 1960, Lexington's population more than doubled, to about 28,000. By 1960, the town had no less than nine Modernist subdivisions.

It was not just convenience, or even the proximity of two of the country's best architecture schools, that made this area a hive of suburban Modernism. It was the culture of the schools at the time. Walter Gropius was chair of architecture at Harvard; his former Bauhaus colleague Marcel Breuer was a professor there until 1946. The dean who hired them, Joseph Hudnut, was so determined to break with tradition that he ordered all Old Master paintings and plaster casts of classical buildings removed from the premises. (With hindsight, this was overkill.) At MIT, meanwhile, William Wurster modernized the design curriculum and hired the Modernist architects Ralph Rapson and Carl Koch. Across the two schools, there was a cohort of people who believed, following the Bauhaus, that art and design disciplines ought to be integrated to express a fundamental unity. They also took up the Bauhaus commitment to designing for the masses. Arguably, however, there was also an openness to experimentation that predated Gropius' influence, evidenced by pioneers like Eleanor Raymond and Edwin Goodell Jr., who built innovative houses in the area in the early 1930s.

So the western edge of Boston saw wave upon wave of idealistic suburb-building. It started with Gropius and Breuer in Lincoln, then moved to Belmont, where Gropius' former student Carl Koch designed his first project, Snake Hill, a handful of houses clinging to rocky ledges that a conventional builder wouldn't touch. The ever-inventive Koch built a boiler house and installed hot-water pipes in the steep road to melt snow and ice. Another Koch venture, Kendal Common in Weston, advertised itself as "Land and an Idea, Community and Modern Architecture," "an adventure in living … building towards a better life." Koch then worked on Conantum, a 100-house neighborhood in Concord designed around a large wetland. Another subdivision, Peacock

Farm (named after its former use), had 50-odd contemporary houses, mostly split-levels, designed by Walter Pierce. This avant-garde tendency culminated in the mid-1960s, when an architect named Mary Otis Stevens and her husband Thomas McNulty designed an extraordinary house with sculptural concrete walls that curved in and out around a long internal pathway. One could enter this pathway from various points outside. Inside, the house was all free-flowing space, with only two real rooms with doors. The house was later demolished, unfortunately.

In Lexington, fresh from their success with Six Moon Hill, TAC purchased another, larger tract, a former dairy farm, and divided it into sixty-eight lots surrounding twenty acres of common land; this became Five Fields. Here TAC tried to regularize the designs that had evolved on Moon Hill, producing several standard plans (based on 12-foot modules) to which it assigned letters of the alphabet. In the MIT Museum archives in Cambridge, I saw the plans and elevations for the EE house, a split-level with an asymmetric peaked roof, and the F house, a shed-roofed single-story model with two bedrooms. The plans reveal efficient space planning within small footprints and are highly sensitive to the connection to the outdoors. The largest expanses of glass were oriented toward the best views, usually south or west, allowing residents to feel that they were in nature. Many houses at Five Fields were custom-designed, however, because buyers requested modifications.

"The interior designs incorporated many features that were considered superior to those offered in tract houses of the time," as a booklet published on the community's fiftieth anniversary notes, "a pass-through from the entrance to the kitchen, a T hall plan that used little space and provided quick access to all areas, a circulation pattern that did not go through the living room, living room fireplaces, and storage space in the furnace room ... The materials used were also considered superior: oak floors, plaster walls and ceilings, metal window sashes and door bucks, metal sliding closet doors, and large panes of glass." Setbacks from the roads were staggered and orientations varied according to the gentle rises and falls of the land. TAC preserved as many old oak trees as it could and the farm's old stone wall.

Five Fields attracted the same kind of young intellectuals as its predecessor had: The first neighborhood group that formed was one that met to read Ancient Greek together. In the two adjoining ponds on the common land, children caught tadpoles and fed the ducks. Early residents installed an outdoor fireplace and a jungle gym on this land, and in the mid-1950s, a pool. While this seems rather luxurious now—a pool for only 60 households—the pool was built because the young families had sunk all their money into their houses and couldn't afford to go on vacation, and the residents did most of the building themselves. For several years in the 1960s, a Five Fields mother staged annual outdoor Shakespeare performances, starring neighborhood children and featuring elaborate sets and costumes, behind her house.

I visited Five Fields on an overcast spring day. My neighborhood guide was long-time resident Rick Treitman, who lives in a house that was built and inhabited by Hideo Sasaki, the legendary landscape architect and founder of the design firm still operating as Sasaki Associates. Sasaki designed the house with architect Allison Goodwin in the mid-1950s, drawing on his Japanese background for its unusual form: a long, low rectangle meets another rectangle at a right angle and seemingly splits it, and its two halves are both topped by pagoda-style roofs. Originally, Treitman told me, the house had four internal gardens, one for each season of the year.

Treitman and I walked a circuit along Barberry Road, up Field Road, along Concord Avenue, and back down Barberry again, as he pointed out favorite houses and described alterations that had been made over time. I had read beforehand, and it was very clear from our walk, that almost all the houses at Five Fields have been expanded, some significantly. We took a footpath through the common land, stopping to see its newest feature—a high-concept, wood-siding-clad children's play wall designed by architects Michael Schanbacher (a Five Fields resident) and Brandon Clifford—before returning to Treitman's house. It, too, is substantially larger than when first built. Treitman and his architect, Eugene Racek, placed another rectangular volume on top of the one that bisects the "split" volume, giving this addition the same distinctive Japanese roof that Sasaki and Goodwin used below.

In the kitchen, we sat down with Treitman's neighbors Sally Bowie and Bob Rotberg and, over wine and cheese, talked about life in Five Fields. Rotberg, a retired professor at Harvard's Kennedy School of Government and a renowned expert on conflict prevention and resolution, moved into his house in 1970. He and his wife had visited friends at Five Fields, and Lexington had excellent schools, so they bought it sight unseen. "The man who owned the house before me was a world-famous cognitive psychologist," he recalled. "We discovered, in coming to see the house that we bought without seeing the inside—because it was just a perfect location and we knew the grounds—that there were Swedish graduate students who had been renting the house, and trashing it, and sunbathing naked on the roof. We had to kick them out, and eventually burn their mattresses."

For Rotberg, Five Fields is a community rather than a neighborhood, an important distinction. "There's something very special that's carried on generation to generation, of people pulling together, and not worrying about creed, religion, politics, and really believing in each other. Because we have an annual meeting, because we have a pool, because we have the common land, it works." Five Fields throws an annual New Year's party, which rotates around residents' houses, and there's still a square dance every fall, a tradition that goes back decades. Regular cleanup days bring residents to the common land with chainsaws, and they make bonfires out of the brush they collect. Local parents even run their own summer camp on the common.

The sense of belonging among Five Fielders struck me as unusually strong, but similar in kind to what you might find in a more conventional, tight-knit suburban neighborhood. But the longer we sat around the table, the more I sensed there was a difference. Sally Bowie, who has lived in Five Fields since 1995, hosts yoga and Pilates classes in her home across the street from Treitman's. She and her husband built a large room on the top of their house—she calls it "the dojo"—and professional teachers come every week to instruct a handful of regulars, all but one of them Five Field residents. This has been going on for eighteen years. "It's a great feeling to hear the laughter [from upstairs when] I'm downstairs reading the paper," Bowie, a licensed clinical social worker, told me. "It just feels nice to have that happening in the house." How many suburbanites devote whole parts of their homes to quasi-public use?

Five Fields reunions have become major events. For its fortieth anniversary in 1992, two residents baked and froze twenty 14-by-14-inch carrot cakes over an entire winter, then combined them into one 8-foot-long cake, decorated with a detailed topographical map of the community. "Roads were made of fruit leather, trees of gumdrops, houses of caramels cut to shape, green frosting for lawns and blue for the pond and swimming pool," according to the anniversary booklet. For the fiftieth reunion, Treitman said, "the thing that I remember is, all of the people who are documented [living] here came back. People came from London and California. People flew in from all over the world—because they remembered this as the best place they'd ever lived."

When I asked Treitman, Bowie, and Rotberg whether Five Fields had changed over the years, Rotberg noted that Lexington has grown slowly in recent decades, unlike many suburban towns. But Bowie had a different answer: "The community has changed, because it costs so much more money to move here."

Built to put high-quality Modernist architecture within reach of families just starting out, Six Moon Hill and Five Fields have come to an ironic fate: The $17,000 and $22,000 houses now sell for well upwards of $1 million. This is in large part a reflection of regional economics. The Boston area has been on an upward climb of prosperity since the early days of TAC, and it has flourishing IT, biotech, and financial sectors in addition to being a higher-education powerhouse. As a result, the metropolitan area has become one of the most expensive in the country in which to rent or buy a home. Lexington, convenient to Cambridge and the tech corridor of Route 128, and still boasting first-rate public schools, is one of the most desirable places in the region. In 2017, the median home sales price in Lexington was $1.15 million. A house in Five Fields sold for $1.36 million in 2017; a Moon Hill house sold for $1.5 million the year before.

It's sad that an egalitarian experiment has devolved into a luxury good. But it's worth considering what has made Five Fields and Moon Hill so sought after, because the high home values are more than just a ripple effect. I heard story after story of people who encountered these communities, by chance or through a personal connection, and fell in love with them—Treitman, for one. An entrepreneur-in-residence at Adobe, Treitman has "an architecture jones" that he traces back to a grad-school stint working at Design Research, the famed Modernist home-goods store in Harvard Square. (In fact, Design Research was founded by Ben Thompson, a member of TAC and Moon Hill resident, specifically to outfit these new, smaller houses with furniture that suited them.) Treitman learned about TAC's Lexington enclaves from a coworker. After he and his wife decided to move to Lexington from the nearby town of Newton, he told the real-estate agent: "Moon Hill, Five Fields, or nothing." When the Sasaki house came on the market, they bought it on the spot.

Something crucial that the members of TAC understood was the importance of designing for children. There's a reason this period was called the Baby Boom: children were in the majority at Five Fields and Six Moon Hill. At one point in the early 1960s, there were ninety-six children on Moon Hill, far eclipsing the number of adults. The Fletchers eventually had four children, and the Harknesses, seven. TAC was highly unusual for two of its seven architects being women, and not just women, but mothers of young children. (This is almost as rare in architecture firms today, unfortunately.) As is clear from their earlier living arrangement, both Sally Harkness and Jean Fletcher were interested in creating a domestic realm that stretched beyond the nuclear family for social support.

In its feature article, *Vogue* described Moon Hill as a paradise for children, a "magnificent exclusive jungle gym" with children's artwork hanging on walls and girls shinnying up lally columns. Many of TAC's Lexington houses had playrooms; some had children's bedrooms that could be separated or combined via a folding wall, and others had built-in homework desks. More importantly, the de-emphasis on the family backyard and generous provision of shared open space drew children outdoors *together*, to play ball games, build forts, and camp out in tents in warm weather. Large windows made it easy to see if a playmate was at home (that is, if the curtains were open). While a bucolic suburb was not as stimulating as the city in many respects, children here could be fairly independent, because they had places to go that were safe, yet not directly under their parents' gaze. In this respect, Six Moon Hill and Five Fields carried on one of the principles of Greenbelt, with its shared courts and lake for independent yet safe playing. Children could even walk to school. But TAC's developments were more or less islands. The Lexington neighborhoods conformed to the use-separating, women-and-children-isolating pattern of suburbanization rather than trying to stop it, as the Garden City and later New Towns did.

The share of American households with children dropped sharply from 1970 to 2012, from 40 percent to 20 percent, and women who have children don't have as many as they used to. America looks different now. But it's striking that nowhere seems designed with children in mind anymore, whether suburban neighborhoods, with big, fenced yards instead of parks, or urban apartment buildings with mostly studio and one-bedroom units, and fitness rooms, but no playrooms. Perhaps for this reason, the number of children at Six Moon Hill and Five Fields has shot up again in recent years, after a period of decline as Baby Boomers' children grew up and moved out. Several residents told me that they are wonderful places to raise kids. Parallel child-rearing, with even a limited degree of cooperation (not as much as Sally Harkness had envisaged in her shared house in Cambridge), ironically seems to provide at least some of the glue that celibacy, religiosity, and semi-isolation provided in Economy.

Given land prices in many suburban areas today, replicating TAC's formula would only result in enclaves of the uber-rich. Of course, that hasn't stopped people from trying. In the Bay Area, there's a development called Walden Monterey currently being built on the scenic Monterey Peninsula, more than an hour south of San Francisco. For the design of the twenty-odd houses, the developer has engaged award-winning architects. The finished development will be gorgeous, but highly exclusive, a weekend retreat for tech executives. Homesites cost $5 million. This Walden will have gates (seriously).

A new suburban neighborhood of single-family homes designed by a leading architects or architects hardly pencils out now at a fairy high price point, let alone at prices affordable for the middle class. Not to mention the environmental toll of greenfield development: Building on an undeveloped, farther-out site means more infrastructure to maintain and more vehicle miles traveled, which increases carbon emissions. That's true even if the homes are designed to use net-zero energy (as the ones at Walden Monterey are). Better to take the spirit of Six Moon Hill and use it to fill gaps in the existing suburban or urban fabric. Architect Barbara Bestor has done this with Blackbirds, a cluster of eighteen houses in the Echo Park neighborhood of L.A., completed in 2015. Bestor took advantage of a city ordinance allowing lots to be subdivided for multiple smaller residences. Some of the houses in Blackbirds are attached into duplex and triplex combinations, while others are freestanding. The interior courtyard of the development is a Dutch *woonerf*, a multi-use space where kids can play, drivers can slowly come in and out, and neighbors can gather.

The need to rethink the suburban home has become urgent as more people age in place, often alone, and as multigenerational households become common once again. (Twenty percent of the population now lives in a multigenerational household, up from 12 percent in 1980; among Asians and Hispanics, the shares are 29 and 27 percent, respectively.) The inventiveness that TAC brought to the single-family home plan lives on in the work of O'Neill Rose, a small Brooklyn architecture firm. Its Choy House (2014) is in Flushing, Queens, one of the most ethnically and racially diverse areas in New York City, on a suburban-style street of modest two-story homes. The firm's client wanted a home that could accommodate not just his immediate family, but his brother's family and his elderly mother. Architects Devin O'Neill and Faith Rose articulated three separate dwellings within one contemporary gable-roofed house. The client, his wife, and their children live on the first and second floors, while a slice of the front of the house is occupied by the client's brother and his wife. The grandmother lives on the lower level, which opens up to a sunken terraced garden. A ground-floor family room is shared by all.

Despite zoning hurdles and initial skepticism from neighbors, the Choy House was a success, and locals came around. "It's like every project you do—no matter what, your immediate neighbor is always going to be kind of upset. They have to live through what you're doing," O'Neill told me. But, he continued, "We had amazing feedback when it was done. People in the neighborhood were really excited about it. We got calls to do the exact same thing on Queens and Long Island."

Still, neither Blackbirds nor the Choy House can be said to have brought high-quality architecture to the masses. (The cheapest home in Blackbirds was listed at $795,000.) For anything like that to happen, architects will have to get creative not just about design solutions, but about their own role and the services they provide. In the 1920s, the United States had something called the Architects' Small House Service Bureau, which produced low-cost stock plans for modest houses; it offered more than 250 (fairly conservative) designs to appeal to different tastes and reflecting regional traditions. "Recognizing the potential profitability to the profession, the American Institute of Architects officially sponsored the bureau, even though some members disavowed this endorsement of standardized designs," writes historian Gwendolyn Wright. A few decades later, Charles Goodman, the designer of Virginia's Hollin Hills, collaborated with the large homebuilder National Homes to offer Modernist standard house plans, which thousands of consumers around the country used to build their own homes. He was sneered at by colleagues as "the production house architect," but chose to wear the label with pride.

The architecture profession's abandoning of this populist approach has resulted in its being sidelined from the decisions that ordinary Americans make about where and how to live. To re-connect architecture with the suburban public, an Australian critic, Rory Hyde, has proposed a "Small Homes Adaptability Service" like the Small House Service Bureau or Australia's midcentury analog, the Small Homes Service, but that "would be geared toward adapting the existing housing stock to suit the needs of today and creating new opportunities to share space and resources." He imagines it performing deft, surgical interventions to the spaces in and around the suburban home:

> It would adapt and join adjacent triple garages into co-working spaces and workshops, shared by the entire block, to support decentralized working. It would install solar panels and link up existing ones to create local energy smart grids, for charging cars and reducing bills. It would adapt front rooms for childcare and social clubs for the elderly, providing space and structure for the informal systems of care that already operate. … Lightweight digital services could be introduced to facilitate sharing of tools, cars, books and time among neighbours. The simplest intervention might be to knock down a fence between dwellings, creating a new semipublic realm of shared facilities, from swimming pools to basketball hoops.

Both pragmatic and exciting, this vision of the future of architecture comes down to the ethos of Six Moon Hill: no fences.

CHAPTER 5

INTEGRATING THE SUBURBS AT "CHECKERBOARD SQUARE"

Concord Park, Trevose, Pennsylvania

Photograph of neighbors walking together from *Ebony* article on Concord Park, February 1957

Photograph of monthly neighborhood meeting at Concord Park, from *Ebony*, February 1957

Morris Milgram papers [Coll. 2176], Historical Society of Pennsylvania

With its Lexington projects, TAC posed a bold architectural alternative to the houses in mass-market housing tracts. It deviated from the suburban norm by keeping the landscape semi-wild and dedicating a higher-than-usual proportion of land to common use. But Six Moon Hill and Five Fields didn't challenge the stark racial segregation of the greater Boston area in the middle of the twentieth century, despite the presence of Hideo Sasaki and a few other nonwhite residents.

As construction began on Five Fields, a builder in the Philadelphia area was trying to reform the suburbs from the opposite direction: He would stick to orthodox architecture and neighborhood planning, but the racial composition of his community would be anything but. His name was Morris Milgram.

Concord Park, in Trevose, Pennsylvania, was one of the first private, integrated housing developments in the country, established years before the 1968 Fair Housing Act would make racial discrimination in housing against the law. It was Milgram's initial venture after setting up as a homebuilder. He wanted to prove that multiracial suburbs were not only possible, but superior to segregated ones. From its groundbreaking in 1954 well into the 1960s and beyond, Concord Park's fortunes were tracked by progressive activists, scholars, and journalists (most of them friendly, but not all). Milgram was to devote the rest of his career to building, promoting, and managing integrated housing. Although he is largely forgotten today, he counted among his early supporters Martin Luther King, Jr., Eleanor Roosevelt, and many other prominent figures of the time.

In *Shelley v. Kraemer* (1948), the Supreme Court had ruled that racially restrictive covenants, such as those Bill Levitt had put in place at his first mega-development on Long Island, could not be enforced by the courts. But the decision did little to change real-estate practices. For one thing, as historian Thomas Sugrue notes, covenants "were more often than not honored in the breach," and did not stop white neighborhoods covered by covenants from "turning over" racially once a black family or two had moved in. More significantly, the federal government and the courts continued to treat as sacrosanct the right of homebuilders—private actors—to choose the occupants of their communities. In 1952 and 1953, the NAACP vigorously lobbied U.S. Steel (which operated the Fairless Hills plant near the Pennsylvania Levittown) to pressure Levitt to change his whites-only sales policy. According to a NAACP attorney, Levitt said that he "could not take a chance on admitting Negroes and then not being able to sell his houses." NAACP officials even raised the issue in a meeting with President Eisenhower in early 1954, but to no avail.

It was in this context that Milgram—an active member of Philadelphia-area civil rights groups—decided to build what the FHA and Levitt family would not. Milgram was going to offer a similar house with similar decor to black and white buyers, at a similar price point. He was going to beat Bill Levitt at his own game.

Milgram was born in New York City in 1916, one of six children of Russian Jewish parents who worked in the garment industry. Growing up on the Lower East Side among Russian and Eastern European immigrants, he imbibed left-wing politics. "At six, I was carried on my sisters' boy friends' shoulders to Socialist picnics," he told a writer for the *New York Post*.

After joining the Socialist Party, the seventeen-year-old Milgram enrolled in City College and became a campus activist. CCNY had been derisively dubbed "the little red school house" by the Hearst press for the radicalism of its students, and in October 1934, Milgram was among those who protested the college administration hosting a reception for student delegates from Benito Mussolini's regime. Milgram and twenty other students were expelled. He switched to Dana College in New Jersey (now Rutgers University) and finished his degree in economics there. At twenty-one, he married Grace Smelo, a young woman from suburban Philadelphia who had graduated from Antioch College in Ohio; they had met while campaigning for Socialist presidential candidate Norman Thomas. Both joined the staff of the Workers Defense League.

Recalling his inspiration to build integrated housing, Milgram often cited a long poem by WDL colleague (and lifelong friend), Pauli Murray. "Dark Testament," first published in 1943, so enthralled Milgram that he read it out loud to audiences around the country. In his 1977 book *Good Neighborhood*, Milgram wrote that after one of those readings:

> I finally realized that the following lines about the sons of slave traders told us that the ghetto's purpose is to preserve the unfreedom blacks suffered under slavery:
>
> Traders still trade in double-talk
> Though they've swapped the selling block
> For ghetto and gun!

> It was then that I resolved to do all I could to end the unwritten law that virtually all new and decent housing was for whites only.

In multiple interviews and letters, Milgram mentioned the influence of "Dark Testament" on him, so there is no reason to doubt its electric effect. However, there were also more prosaic factors involved in his career change. In 1946, Milgram and Grace had their first child, Gene, and soon looked to shore up their finances. "[W]e had decided that ten years service with the WDL was as much sacrifice as the growing family could afford at this time," Milgram noted in the family's 1947 holiday letter.

Grace's father, William Smelo, was a homebuilder, and he asked his son-in-law to join his firm. After repeated invitations, Milgram finally agreed, on the condition that "[Melo's] firm would back me financially in my efforts to develop integrated housing, if I would learn the business." Milgram started in the summer of 1947. "For four and a half years I thus built houses for whites only while my conscience hurt," he wrote.

In 1952, after becoming company president on the death of his father-in-law, Milgram was ready. He made a decisive break with the old business, announcing his intentions rather dramatically at a meeting of the Philadelphia Mayor's Commission on Human Relations. ("I ... told the group I would rather be a laborer and live in a slum than build housing for whites only.")

He struggled to find backers for his still-nebulous project. After many fruitless months, the American Friends Service Committee, a Quaker activist group, introduced him to George Otto. Otto was a more conventional, and successful, builder who was sympathetic to Milgram's thinking. They formed a stock corporation and sold shares to their friends and associates.

Without Otto, it's very possible that Concord Park would never have been built. "Otto brought to the Concord Park project an established reputation for 'sound business thinking' and probity, as well as a highly respected Quaker name … thus lending an aura of respectability to an otherwise radical idea," as two historians of integrated housing wrote. The new corporation handpicked a board of directors, six white and three black men; two of the latter were physicians, and the third a former president of Florida A&M College. They bought two tracts with the funding they had raised: fifty acres in Bucks County, just over the Philadelphia line, for $100,000, and nine acres in Northeast Philadelphia for $22,200.

By August 1954, when sales for Concord Park opened, the total stock offering of $150,000 had been subscribed by sixty-five investors. (Quakers and socialists were the easiest to convince, Milgram said.) Securing mortgage financing, however, proved next to impossible. After more than twenty banks turned Milgram down, a New York bank with experience lending to blacks agreed to take on some of the mortgages, breaking the dam and effectively rescuing the whole enterprise.

"EASY TO OWN … DELIGHTFUL TO LIVE IN," proclaimed a sales sheet for "THE ARIZONA," a simple ranch house fringed by trees and shrubs, shown in a black-and-white sketch. "You'll find CONCORD PARK the perfect community for careful buyers," the sales copy continued, "providing the freedom of country life … the privacy of a ¼ acre lot … the facilities of a large city, only minutes away."

In late 1954 and early '55, prospective homebuyers drove north from Philly on Roosevelt Boulevard, a quarter-mile past the city line, then forked left at the drive-in movie theater to reach what was becoming Concord Park. Most did not know there was an unincorporated black suburb called Linconia close by, which black Philadelphians had settled from the 1920s. Linconia's homes were modest and self-built, because residents could not obtain loans for construction, and early on, the Ku Klux Klan had burned a cross there.

In a muddy field stood Concord Park's first phase—twenty-nine houses newly finished or under construction. Stepping into the model home, visitors found a comforting ambience of conventional, middle-class domesticity. The 19-foot-long living room, looking out on the back yard, had a framed picture of Lake Shore Drive, plant stands, and a coffee table bearing ceramic ashtrays. The boy's bedroom had books and gadgets; the girl's, an easel and a rocker. Sales agents pointed out modern features like a garbage disposal and pre-tuned TV antenna, and they talked up the floor plan, which allowed kids to troop from their bedrooms into the kitchen and outside without crossing (and dirtying) the living room.

For all the community's tract-suburb character, Milgram and his partners had not skimped on its design. The house plans were drawn up by William H. Roberts, soon to become a respected landscape architect and a founding partner of the firm Wallace, McHarg, Roberts & Todd. The builders brought in a respected New York stylist, Beatrice West, to decorate the model home. That decision reflected Milgram's belief in the power of merchandising, but also his instinct that attractive design and good amenities could eclipse "the possibilities of identification as 'that integrated community'" which would hurt sales. The hiring of West had a political edge. A few years earlier, as Milgram was aware, she had styled the six models at Levittown, Pennsylvania, several miles east of Concord Park.

Some 25,000 people toured the Concord Park model in the first four months that it was open. Ninety-five percent of them were white. Milgram's company had placed ads in the local papers, not indicating the open-occupancy principle of the development. It had also sent out 20,000 pieces of direct mail to members of liberal groups, urging them to put their money where their beliefs were. The builders left promotion in the black community to word of mouth, which turned out a few thousand prospective black visitors, not nearly as many as the white prospects. But the first stage of Concord Park's *sales* contradicted this pattern completely. By Christmas 1954, Milgram had about fifty deposits from black families—and only ten from whites.

There were a few reasons for this. First, the disparity in housing choice for whites and blacks at the time was stark. All around Concord Park, new communities like Levittown and Fairless Hills beckoned white buyers; they could comparison-shop, which is why Milgram did not stint on extra features like a built-in laundry hamper. For black would-be suburbanites, the situation was very different. Between 1946 and 1953, 140,000 new homes were built in the Philadelphia area; just 1,044 of these—less than one percent—were available to blacks. Concord Park was the only option.

When white customers learned about the "open occupancy" policy, if they didn't turn on their heels and leave (some did, most didn't), they asked what the ultimate racial balance would be. The sales team told them it would be about 80 percent white and 20 percent black, reflecting area demographics. But whites were skeptical. "This explanation failed to satisfy many whites, especially those who recognized the tremendous pressure of the 550,000 blacks in the nine-county Greater Philadelphia area who could not buy … at any of the hundreds of new developments then being built," Milgram wrote. Fearful of moving into a neighborhood that would quickly become majority-black, and the declining home values that would ensue, they went elsewhere.

This was, of course, the very last thing that Milgram wanted. His shining example of integration was off to a rocky start. "One night, I woke up sweating," he recounted to the Catholic magazine *Sign* in the late Sixties. "'Morris, you idiot,' I told myself, 'you're building another Negro ghetto as sure as Bilbo.'" (He was referring to Theodore Bilbo, the stridently racist Mississippi politician who once called for the deportation of black Americans.)

Something had to be done. At a board meeting in early 1955, member Jane Reinheimer, a white AFSC housing activist, broached a controversial idea: a quota. Several people bristled. (One black board member later said he found quotas "undemocratic.") But others argued that such a drastic measure was necessary. A rigged housing market left them no choice but to employ aggressive tactics toward its dismantling. Or as one historian puts it, "Milgram and Otto found it necessary to employ their own microscopic version of the federal government's illiberal market controls to fight the very effects of the government's policies in the first place."

By a narrow margin, the board agreed to the quota plan. According to Milgram, he had suggested a 50/50 split, but William Gray, the former Florida A&M president, adjusted it "to prevent formation of a black majority" and therefore, presumably, to ease whites' fears. The ratio of white to black buyers was set at 55 to 45 percent. Milgram hung a map of Concord Park in his office, inserting red and blue pins in it to represent black and white buyers. By 1958, all 139 houses had been sold and the target ratio had been met, thanks in large part to the efforts of a salesman named Stuart Wallace.

The first two couples to move into Concord Park were George and Eunice Grier, a research psychologist and a publicist for a Quaker organization, both white, and Charles and Virginia Henry, a machine operator and bookkeeper, both black. Never one to miss a PR opportunity, Milgram organized an open house in November 1954 that was more press conference than kaffee klatsch, with government officials, activists, and reporters in attendance. An "afternoon tea" at the Griers' home a few months later served as the basis of an enthusiastic article in *House & Home*.

There were several interracial couples at Concord Park, a few communists, and many nonconformists. Black households had higher incomes than their white counterparts—a feature of many early integrated housing developments, likely due to the difficulty blacks faced in getting mortgages even with good incomes and credit. The subdivision's many children played together, while their parents formed a babysitting co-op and bowling, photography, and sewing clubs, like the residents of any other "cookie-cutter" suburb. In 1957, when William and Daisy Myers became the first black residents of Levittown, provoking angry mobs, Concord Park dispatched an interracial group to stand watch over their house.

"SUBURB BREAKS RACIAL BARRIER," the *New York Times* announced on its front page on March 10, 1957. "New Private Housing Project at Philadelphia Integrates Negroes and Whites - NO INCIDENTS OCCUR - Not a Family Has Moved From Colony That Ideals and Tenacity Built." Against the odds, Milgram had done it.

In 1956, the Milgram family, which now included a daughter named Elizabeth, moved into a new house a few miles away from Concord Park. Greenbelt Knoll was a much smaller development—only nineteen homes—that Milgram and Otto built concurrently with Concord Park, on the little tract they had purchased near the northeast border of Philadelphia. It differed from Concord Park, though, in ways that are telling.

Here, Milgram sought avant-garde architecture, engaging the local firm Montgomery & Bishop. Robert Bishop was a Quaker and had co-founded Bryn Gweled, an intentional, interracial community in Bucks County; it is easy to imagine him meeting Milgram or Otto socially. He also taught at the University of Pennsylvania, and that affiliation may have been what brought the famed Modernist Louis Kahn into the project. Bishop led the design of Greenbelt Knoll and Kahn consulted on it, although the extent of his involvement is hazy.

The houses that Bishop (and Kahn and another consultant, Harry Duncan) designed were long, low volumes that burrowed into the site's terrain. Clad in wood siding, they had 27-foot-long windows and flat roofs. The designers, with landscape architect Margaret Lancaster Duncan, the went to great lengths to accommodate existing trees, cutting a hole in the roof of a breezeway in one case. This deference to nature points to the influence of Frank Lloyd Wright on Bishop, who had been a fellow at Wright's Taliesen for three years. Greenbelt Knoll's homes were significantly more expensive than those at Concord Park, priced at $22,500 and up for three- and five-bedroom homes. Of the nineteen houses, eight were sold to black buyers, or 42 percent.

Greenbelt Knoll verged on an intentional community—it was a speculative development, but one so small that Milgram could almost fill it by calling the numbers in his address book. Its marketing leaflets looked "arty" and touted a design award from the American Institute of Architects. This was an urban enclave for progressive members of the upper middle class, skewing intellectual: one resident was Charles Fuller, a playwright who later won a Pulitzer Prize; another was the pastor, civil rights leader, and anti-apartheid activist Leon Sullivan.

These differences throw Concord Park into sharper relief as a mass-market demonstration of integrated housing and doppelgänger to Levittown. As such, it was more unusual than Greenbelt Knoll, which had analogs such as Hollin Hills in Virginia. In November 1964, Concord Park celebrated its tenth anniversary with a dinner-dance at a Marriott Motor Lodge in Bala Cynwyd; it must have been the only homeowner association event featuring a speech by national civil-rights leader Bayard Rustin. But its thoroughgoing suburban character was one reason why it began to diverge from Milgram's vision, around the same time as the festive tenth anniversary dinner-dance.

———————

Milgram wanted Concord Park to remain integrated. To that end, he asked owners to sign agreements giving his company the right to sell the home to the buyer of its choosing (a mechanism to ensure that black and white residents remained in equilibrium). After an early round of resales of this nature, time and market dynamics took hold. Black housing demand was still strong. But in the 1960s and 1970s, Levittown-style suburbs and their "ticky-tacky" houses fell out of favor with many liberal whites. Concord Park became majority-black. In 2000, the last of its original white inhabitants, Warren and Betsy Swartzbeck, moved out, an event covered by the national press as the death of Morris Milgram's dream.

Milgram's vision for Concord Park may seem romantic now, but driving around the place, nothing about it suggests failure. Houses are occupied and well-tended, and many have been added onto. Ironically, as a predominantly black subdivision, Concord Park has ended up solving the "housing problem" for more black people than when it first opened.

Joyce Hadley, who is black, grew up in Concord Park, and except for one seven-year stint away, she has lived there ever since. Now an unofficial ambassador for the neighborhood as well as a local official with the Democratic Party, Hadley invited me to her home—her childhood home, in fact—on Concord Drive one Saturday for an interview. After showing me around the "California" model (extensively renovated, but with still-working radiant heating in the floors), she told me about her parents and childhood. Her father, from Thomasville, Georgia, was an insurance underwriter with the Veterans Administration who had served in the segregated Army. Her mother's parents immigrated from Barbados to Philadelphia, where her mother grew up. Joyce's mother, Marjorie, had an independent streak. As a teenager, she shocked her deeply Anglican parents by converting to Catholicism. (Joyce and her two siblings were raised Catholic.) In the Sixties, when popular music was shaking the world, Marjorie listened instead to opera, which she adored: Puccini, Verdi.

"She liked to take risk; she liked to explore everything," Joyce told me over a plate of cookies in her dining room. "She never felt isolated in any particular group because she happened to be African American. She went everywhere. That was one of the reasons she liked the idea of moving into a neighborhood such as Concord Park." Joyce's father learned about Concord Park through his underwriting work at the VA, and they moved there in 1956, when Joyce was in third grade. Hearing Joyce talk about her mother with a photograph of the (very beautiful) Marjorie on the table next to her, I sensed the strong-mindedness, even stubbornness, that would have motivated some early residents of Concord Park. Moving to an integrated suburb was the opposite of the path of least resistance.

Joyce's brother George, an assistant principal at Bensalem High School, bought a house across the street and lived there until his death in 2012. Now that house is owned by a couple that is half Nigerian, half Ukrainian, Joyce noted. Since the early 2000s, "things have changed," she said. "Morris Milgram would be happy, because we have an Asian population that's here, we have a Latino population here, we have African here, we have Caucasian here. So it's turning back" to integration.

Those who grew up in Milgram's neighborhoods when integration was rare say the experience shaped them. "It affected me for my whole life," his son, Gene Milgram, said. He remembers a particular interaction that took place in Greenbelt Knoll when he was young boy. "We were living in Number 5. The man who moved into Number 3 was the highest-ranking black firefighter in Philly, Roosevelt Barlow. I remember having a conversation with him one day: 'So why'd you move here?' He proceeded to explain that he was living somewhere else in Philly and that he couldn't buy a house, that builders wouldn't sell a house to a black person. He said to me, 'They wouldn't take my money.' My reaction was, 'But that's crazy!'"

David Fuller, one of the children of playwright Charles Fuller, still lives in the family home in Greenbelt Knoll. "We were a tight-knit block," he says. "The neighbors knew the children, the children knew the neighbors. Everybody's eyes on everybody." Now, Longford Street is more mixed than Milgram could have imagined, with Asian and gay families. Fuller says he wouldn't live anywhere else: "I'm a youth detention counselor in West Philadelphia. When I leave that job and come home, it's like I'm stepping out of my work skin into peace and quiet. In the wintertime when it snows, it looks like Narnia out here ... I love the peacefulness; I love the fact that my two children and my wife will be able to see what I saw as a child."

In retrospect, both the methods and goals of the open-housing movement invite criticism. Milgram felt torn about using quotas, never quite convincing himself that the end justified the means. Quotas gave easy ammunition to segregationists, allowing them to paint the open-housing project as "totalitarian" on the one hand, or capricious on the other—one Deerfield opponent of Milgram's sneeringly referred to his "little game of racial chess." Although cries of social engineering provided useful cover for racism, the heavy-handedness of advocates' methods did make many people, white and black, uneasy.

The movement emphasized squeaky-clean communities— photogenic idylls of racial harmony. Concord Park, notably, provided significantly fewer homes to blacks than if the houses had simply been sold to the first would-be buyers, who were almost all black. (George Otto had in fact proposed this course, but Milgram and other board members of both races dissuaded him.) Striking an "ideal" racial balance meant turning qualified black buyers away, a contradictory thing for civil rights activists to be doing. And given that black homeowners at these developments often earned more money than their white neighbors (because of the intense black demand for housing and builders' insistence on finding exemplary black residents), it can be argued that living in these places let whites feel good about themselves for consorting with blacks of a higher social status than their own, thereby distracting them from class and power inequities between white and black America writ large.

Assuaging white fears was at the heart of the open-housing theory of change. Social progress was seen as hinging on white people coming around——an idea that now seems naive and too accepting of institutionalized racism as a fact of life.

Yet it would be wrong to see open housing, and Milgram's crusade, as cop-outs or failures. Decades on, the social science research embraced by Milgram and his cohort has shown time and again that housing is central to matters of equity in America. Where we live does indeed shape our destinies. The homeownership rate for nonwhite Americans still lags that of whites, and the wealth accrued from homeownership by whites over generations is a major factor in the stark and persistent racial wealth gap. In identifying housing as a—or the—key concern, open-housing advocates were ahead of their time. "Housing is everybody's problem," Milgram wrote.

Fifty years later, the kinds of neighborhoods Milgram imagined as the next rung on the ladder of progress are more prevalent, but far from widespread. Systemic racism endures (in, for example, the discriminatory mortgage lending practices implicated in the crash of 2008). Nor has white prejudice evaporated—it has proved extremely stubborn. Once a racial minority in a neighborhood reaches a certain threshold, whites are still likely to decamp, research has shown. Racial and economic segregation in public schools is actually getting worse. Although suburbia has diversified considerably, whites still drive the real-estate market, given their overall majority and disproportionate housing wealth. That means majority-minority suburbs, being less attractive to whites, tend to have lower property values, furthering the pattern of inequity. Plans to locate affordable housing or homeless shelters in affluent (usually majority-white) neighborhoods often meet opposition as fierce as that in Deerfield in 1960, with eerily similar objections to "the process" and disavowal of any bias.

Now, it has become clear that the only thing that would redress the inequities in housing wealth between blacks and whites would be a muscular policy intervention. In the meantime, it wouldn't hurt if more white Americans of means followed Milgram's law. Bill Levitt said of his exclusion of blacks from the Levittowns, "We can solve a housing problem, or we can solve a racial problem, but we cannot combine the two." Morris Milgram knew they were inextricable.

In the years since Milgram's death, his name has fallen into obscurity. But his legacy is carried on by a handful of American fair-housing groups, such as the Oak Park Regional Housing Center in Oak Park, Illinois, a jurisdiction of 52,000 that borders Chicago on the west. A streetcar suburb that boomed in the early twentieth century, Oak Park is known for its large collection of Frank Lloyd Wright buildings (including Wright's own home and studio) and its air of liberal affluence. But it does more than pay lip service to integration. In the 1960s, when racial steering and blockbusting caused massive white flight on Chicago's west side, residents of Oak Park acted to preempt the same fate. They passed a local fair-housing ordinance and, in 1972, established the housing center. The center works directly with apartment seekers—rentals make up 40 percent of the town's housing stock—to counter patterns of residential segregation.

Oak Park is 67 percent white, 21 percent black, 8 percent Hispanic or Latino, and 5 percent Asian. Rob Breymaier, who directed the housing center for twelve years until May 2018, told me that many white apartment seekers assume the eastern section of Oak Park (closer to Chicago) must have high crime and bad schools. "The reality is not that," he said. "The reality is [that] pretty much wherever you live in Oak Park, it's just about the same. Oak Park is only 4.5 square miles. There's not a whole lot of variation that could even occur." Staff of the housing center "affirmatively market" neighborhoods in this eastern section and elsewhere, so that Oak Park doesn't end up like so many cities and suburbs—with zones of mostly white affluence, and another zone where low-income African Americans are concentrated. "We don't have a black part of the community that's been left behind, which is typically what happens in diverse but segregated communities," Breymaier said. "What that ends up doing is creating this bigger intentionality in the community, where the value of people regardless of their race is a central tenet of who we are."

I asked Breymaier if people ever express surprise that a proactive approach to integration would be needed half a century after the Fair Housing Act. Isn't this a problem we already solved? "I hear that all the time," he said. But even in Oak Park, he argued, complacency would swiftly undo years of progress. Unconscious biases shape our decisions about where to live—even those of us who self-identify as seeking a diverse neighborhood. "This isn't about people's intentions, or whether they're good or bad people," he said. "If we don't interact with them [at the housing center], biases and stereotypes will win the day." When the center assists households moving into Oak Park, according to Breymaier's analysis of the center's data, 65 to 70 percent of the time, they move in a way that sustains or promotes integration. When the housing center is not involved, that happens less than half the time. "If we weren't here," he concluded, "the community would begin to segregate."

Breymaier conceded that Oak Park is not a utopia by any stretch. "There are feelings from African Americans and Latinos that they're not as valuable," he noted. "Right now, our village trustees are entirely white. We have an identifiable achievement gap in our schools by race." That gap was explored by the recent docuseries *America to Me*, filmed over a year at Oak Park and River Forest High School; among the many points of inequity touched on, black parents say the school doesn't expect excellence from their children, only from white students. Good intentions won't undo the legacy of structural racism. But in the case of the housing center, at least, when channeled into years of hard work, they have made a dent. "Oak Park isn't really that special of a place," Breymaier said. "It's just that we've tried."

CHAPTER 6

THE FIGHT OVER THE SOUL OF A NEW TOWN

Reston, Virginia

Townhouses on Reston's Lake Anne, designed by William Conklin and James Rossant and photographed between 1965 and 1972

A few years ago, on assignment for a magazine, I arranged to interview a filmmaker in Reston, thirty miles from where I live. I hadn't been to Reston since I was a child growing up in another Northern Virginia suburb. After battling traffic on the Washington Beltway, I parked and followed locals on foot through a narrow passageway. When Lake Anne Plaza opened up before me, I stopped, surprised.

A crescent of apartments and shops stood at one end, behind a fountain composed of jostling concrete forms. From there, the plaza hooked around a lake. A high-rise with concrete turrets, on one shore, faced glass-walled townhouses on the other. This romantic Brutalist set piece was the last thing you'd expect to find amid the bland office parks and colonial pastiche of Northern Virginia. It was as if avant-garde architects in the 1960s had come together to build the anti-suburb (which, I learned later, is basically what happened). And in 2016, it wasn't an artifact: it *worked* as public space. Kids climbed over the fountain. An elderly man picked his way through the plaza with a walker. A woman in a headscarf hurried past on her phone, and a mother and her adult daughter chatted in Spanish.

I met the filmmaker, Rebekah Wingert-Jabi, at a French-Vietnamese restaurant on the plaza. Over lunch, she told me she'd lived in cities around the world—Los Angeles, Beijing, and Jerusalem. But nowhere was quite like here, where she'd grown up. So she decided to move back with her Palestinian husband and their small daughter. "There was something about this suburban community in Virginia that was pulling me back," she said. And when she settled in again, "it felt so good. Finally, in my adult life, I don't feel the isolation I felt so many places where I lived."

That was founder Robert E. Simon's aim all along. Simon was the scion of a New York real-estate developer. He grew up in Manhattan, taking long, culture-soaked European vacations with his family. After graduating from Harvard, he spent two months riding a bicycle around Europe, and it was a formative experience. On his bike, instead of being shut up in a car or train, Simon was open to the elements, and to chance encounters with locals. He soaked up the beauty of Italian hill towns and the happy bustle of French market towns. Wherever he went, he saw houses packed tight around a small square or plaza, and the lesson stayed with him.

In 1960, after serving in the Army and running the family business, Simon Enterprises, he sold his 40-percent stake in Carnegie Hall and bought 6,750 acres of farmland well beyond Washington's metropolitan sprawl, in the far west of Fairfax County. There, he determined to build a new kind of development—not a suburb but an anti-suburb, an Italian hill town reinterpreted by great Modernist architects and generously interlaced with nature. Inhabitants of this town would not simply live; they would attain the good life, enjoying a sense of place and close social ties that the tract builders of postwar America had sacrificed in their haste and profit-seeking.

What he'd seen on the bike trip affected him, but Simon didn't arrive at his vision through direct inspiration alone. He was familiar with the legacy of Ebenezer Howard—in fact, he had a personal connection to it. Simon's father had been one of the investors in Radburn, New Jersey, a 1920s experiment in Garden City planning cut short by the Depression. (Radburn was planned by Clarence Stein and Henry Wright, who consulted on Greenbelt.) The younger Simon read the writings of Lewis Mumford, a steadfast advocate for Garden City principles. He even invited Mumford to weigh in on the plans for Reston (Mumford declined).

Carrying on the vision of Greenbelt, Reston anticipated the rediscovery of "walkable urbanism" and mixed-use development by decades. After an early and close brush with failure, it has grown and prospered. But now its residents are engaged in a bitter fight over its future. The question it faces—and that more and more suburbs will face in coming years—is one of identity. Should Reston remain a suburb, or become a city?

———————

Even to members of his immediate family, Simon's choice was baffling. The site of the future town was distant from Washington and Alexandria. It was six miles from a new airport then being built, Dulles International, but there was nothing else in the vicinity of the airport except corn, tobacco, and cows. But Simon saw the location between D.C. and Dulles as strategic.

Before hiring engineers, planners or architects, Simon took out a yellow notepad and jotted down his vision for the town, Reston (the name was a play on his initials, R-E-S). Open spaces, he added. Art. Beauty. "People first."

Simon wanted residents of the town to live in close proximity, in a mix of apartments, townhouses, and detached homes. This would help fulfill one of the guiding principles he set out in Reston's first master plan in 1962: that a Restonian should be able "to remain in a single neighborhood throughout his or her life."

In Reston, he hoped, a young person just starting out could rent a small apartment; when that person married and had children, he or she could move into a detached house nearby. When the children left home, their parents could downsize to a townhouse, also within the same neighborhood. Finally, they might choose to spend their golden years as Simon did, in a Reston apartment with urban conveniences like stores and restaurants at hand.

"As a by-product," Simon wrote, the whole-lifespan neighborhood "also results in the heterogeneity that spells a lively and varied community." Different sizes and styles of homes would prevent the homogeneity that results when a neighborhood is designed solely for two-parent families with young children, as tract suburbs of the 1950s and '60s were. The influence of the Garden City on Reston is clear from another of Simon's seven principles, "That the people be able to live and work in the same community."

Reston was part of the international New Towns movement, which aimed to redirect sprawl development into rational and fully rounded satellite cities. (The New Town was, in essence, the Garden City 2.0.) Reston was inspired by European New Towns, especially Tapiola in Finland and Britain's Stevenage. In the U.S., HUD funded fourteen New Towns, in a range of urban, suburban, and rural locations, in the early 1970s. The program was mostly a failure, not least because the government withdrew its support after a few years. With the exception of The Woodlands in Texas, the other American New Towns that succeeded predated the government's Title VII funding: Reston and Columbia, Maryland, developed by James Rouse.

To his other concerns for Reston, Simon added another that was very much of the zeitgeist. Social scientists in the 1960s were predicting the imminent arrival of "the leisure society." Thanks to technological advances and increased productivity, the theory went, Americans would soon need to work only twenty or thirty hours a week to enjoy the same standard of living, if not a higher one. Of course, that didn't happen. Technological breakthroughs continued, productivity soared, and work weeks only grew longer. But the 1960s-era preoccupation with "the leisure society" helps explain Simon's number-one principle for Reston: "That the widest choice of opportunities be made available for the full use of leisure time."

Reston's original plan knitted together the various strands of Simon's thinking. As master architects and planners, the developer hired the New York firm of Whittlesey and Conklin (later Conklin and Rossant). The firm had a Garden City pedigree: one of its principals had worked on Radburn. To ensure that Reston would have a balance of jobs and houses, and hence not become a dormitory suburb, the planners ran an industrial/research zone east to west along Route 606, bisecting the parcel. On either side of this zone were dotted "village centers," concentrations of commercial, cultural, and recreational facilities. There would be high-density housing in them, too, but this would stretch beyond them as well, forming what the planners called an "urban sinew" throughout the town. Each village center would promote a different kind of leisure activity. The first, Lake Anne, would be for boating and fishing, while Hunters Woods, the second, would have "a horseback riding character," Simon said.

The whole concept was fundamentally at odds with the Fairfax County zoning code, which, like most zoning codes then and now, separated land into distinct single-use categories (agricultural, residential, commercial) and stipulated things like lot sizes and setbacks. Simon knew this from the outset, and with his characteristic confidence, decided the zoning would have to change to fit the plan and not the other way around. He and his staff proposed a new zoning category, Planned Residential Community (PRC), and county officials agreed to it. It's hard to overstate how crucial this legality was—Reston would have been a non-starter under regular zoning—and how influential. Reston's rezoning set the stage for the founding of Columbia, Maryland, a couple of years later, and pointed to the master-planned communities that now dot the suburbs of every American city, however far removed these may be from Restonian ideals.

Simon was determined to make Lake Anne as complete as possible before the first residents moved in, for a few reasons. Given the importance he attached to both leisure and community, he believed that facilities like the golf course and plaza-side shops were not extras, but critical infrastructure, which residents deserved to have at their disposal from the beginning. But he was also selling a way of life that was vastly different from what people could expect in surrounding communities, and he knew that prospective residents would struggle to understand it without a full-scale demonstration. Lake Anne Village Center would need to be Reston in microcosm, a 3-D advertisement and mission statement rolled into one.

The main designers of Lake Anne were James Rossant and Bill Conklin. Both men had studied under Walter Gropius at Harvard and shared his commitment to a socially oriented Modernism. At Lake Anne, riffing on the famous Italian fishing village of Portofino, they wove their village around and between two fingers of water at the northern end of the lake. Next to the northernmost fingertip, they put a J-shaped crescent of shops and dwellings that enfolds a plaza stepping down to the water. Lake Anne Village Center reaches a few stories high, focuses on a public plaza, and hugs its shores, just as Portofino does, but it speaks a different, more bracing architectural language: that of Brutalism, the 1960s and '70s school of Modernism that fancied concrete and monumental or bristling forms.

Rossant and Conklin built their crescent in a soft brown brick accented with horizontal concrete bands. In front of the ground-level shops, concrete columns support two upper stories of townhouses, each bay accentuated by a narrow fin that rises a few feet above the roofline. The townhouses are entered via a concrete stair leading behind the crescent to arched brick doorways.

Despite the modern materials used, the design has a classical flavor, emphasized by the repeating columns and fins. (More than one critic has compared Lake Anne Plaza to the eighteenth-century Royal Crescent at Bath in England.) Across the plaza and down a waterside path stands Heron House, the sixteen-story apartment building where Bob Simon lived in old age.

Two prominent architects from Washington filled in the edges of Lake Anne Village with more small-scale Modernist housing. Charles Goodman, the designer of nearby Hollin Hills, produced Hickory Cluster, ninety townhouses tucked gently into a wooded hillside overlooking the lake. The houses vary in size and height, but they all bear the same grid in front, a concrete frame that is sometimes enclosed with large panes of glass, sometimes left open as a patio. Down the hill and closer to the lake is the pastel-hued Waterview Cluster, another group of ninety townhouses, designed by the trailblazing female architect Chloethiel Woodard Smith. Smith took a different tack from Goodman, translating the architecture of Old World towns like Portofino into a contemporary but more mainstream style.

Reston's first residents moved into Waterview Cluster in December 1964, and a few months later, all the commercial space at Lake Anne Village Center had been leased up. Tenants included a Safeway grocery store, the Lakeside Pharmacy, a Fairfax County branch library, a restaurant, dry cleaners, a barber shop, a Scandinavian home-goods store, and a children's store. A year later, the population had grown to around 500.

Simon and his team held a dedication for Lake Anne on December 4, 1965. It was a "Salute to the Arts," featuring a reading by the poet Stephen Spender. "Fully Planned Town Opens in Virginia," the *New York Times* announced on its front page the next day. Ada Louise Huxtable, the *Times'* architecture critic, hailed Reston as "one of the most striking communities in the country."

There was only one problem: It wasn't selling.

———————

When the first model homes opened in mid-1964, 10,000 people came to see them the initial weekend. They would have started their tour at the sales center, a distinctive round building with orange pull-down shutters. Inside were a scale model of the future town and an exhibit on planned-community living (including slide shows and rotating display posts). When the shutters were up, the window wall looked onto the Fairfax County countryside and construction works.

Chuck Veatch was the third salesman Simon hired for the New Town. At first, there wasn't a lot for him to show except for the model and promotional materials. "We painted a whole lot of word pictures. We talked a lot about the promise of this new way of living," said Veatch, who later moved to Reston and has remained there for half a century. He remembers one night when he stayed late at the sales center. "I was about ready to lock up, and I heard somebody come to the front door. I got all the way around [the circle of the building], and saw this guy in a suit with his tie pulled down, very disheveled-looking. He looked at me and said, 'Holy crap, where am I? I saw this and thought it was a spaceship.'" The man had gotten lost on his way to Dulles airport.

From the sales center, visitors continued to the homes. The range of styles these demonstrated, from Chimney House's Brutalist gothic to Waterview's suburban Neo-Italian, was deliberate on Simon's part. Collectively, he believed, they offered something for everyone, even if one or the other was not to a person's taste. (He referred to them as his "vanilla, chocolate and strawberry" flavors of housing.)

Despite the thousands of visitors on that first weekend, early sales were flat. "[T]he only deposit," Veatch later told a local historian, "… was one left by an over-excited poodle smack in the middle of the king-sized bed" in the Waterview Cluster model. Simon had not stinted on quality, and had given his architects a free hand; as a result, prices had gone up from projections. The development could not compete on price or on location. And the architectural flavors did not, in fact, appeal to everyone. "We felt the resistance to the houses," Veatch recalls. "You had to be a very urban-thinking kind of person to buy into this." Charles Goodman even came to talk to the sales force, and gave them advice on how to answer buyers' questions and concerns about the avant-garde architecture.

Soon enough, the salespeople realized they would be wasting their time appealing to the typical suburban home-shopping family. They focused on the kind of people who intuitively grasped Simon's vision: architects, planners, psychologists, teachers. "The people that bought into Reston were definitely a type," Veatch said. "I still joke: If we saw somebody pull up in a Volvo and get out wearing Birkenstocks, we would fight to see who would get him as a client."

And another group of eager buyers emerged: African Americans. From the outset, Simon had intended that Reston would be open to people of all races and ethnicities. He did not try to achieve an ideal racial balance like Morris Milgram, however, or attempt the level of social engineering of James Rouse, the developer who would build Columbia a couple of years later. "[W]e're not engineering this thing," Simon told an interviewer in 1966. "It's going to happen naturally." It did, probably because demand was so high. A decade after Concord Park, middle-class blacks were still shut out of most of the suburban real-estate market.

Fairfax County real-estate agents would sometimes steer clients away from Reston, but word of mouth and press coverage drew black residents. "Utopian New Town in South is model of modern concepts," proclaimed a headline in *Ebony* in 1966. The magazine devoted a five-page feature to the town and some of its early black residents, including the families of a State Department attorney and a high-school principal.

Laura Thomas, who is African American and originally from New York City, was living in Washington in 1964 when her husband suggested they drive out to see a new place he had seen an ad for, in Fairfax County. They had been trying to buy a house in the Maryland suburbs, but had been turned down repeatedly, even when they offered to buy one home outright with no mortgage. Virginia, a Southern state where interracial marriage was still against the law, hardly seemed more promising.

"No one wanted to go across the bridge. Nobody," Thomas remembers. "I had an uncle and an aunt who lived in Culpeper. I knew what Virginia was like. I was not going to Virginia." But Thomas was disappointed by the public schools in Washington and wanted to move to a place where her children could get a good education. She agreed to the drive. Not long after, the Thomases purchased a house in Reston.

Because Simon was determined to make Reston a fully-rounded community as quickly as possible, construction happened on several fronts at the same time, and fast. By Lake Anne's dedication day, Simon had already finished an 18-hole golf course, a stable for the second, equestrian-themed village (Hunters Woods), two swimming pools, four tennis courts, a number of playgrounds, and several miles of pedestrian walkways, as well as hundreds of units of housing—not to mention the village center itself.

All this expenditure strained the resources—and patience—of Simon's main backer, the oil company Gulf. In 1967, its subsidiary Gulf Reston took over the day-to-day running of the project. The board pressured Simon to resign as chairman. He refused, and he was fired. He moved back to New York.

Three years into its existence, the town had lost its visionary. The new bosses abandoned avant-garde architecture and ramped up production of single-family houses, at a higher volume and lower price point than Simon intended. Sales improved.

Lake Anne is a paradox: The embodiment of Simon's dream

and of the pioneers' leap of faith, it defines Reston. Yet as the years passed, it also became anomalous. Under Gulf Reston and, later, Mobil (which bought the 3,700 acres of then-undeveloped land in the late 1970s), Reston grew along much more suburban lines, with cul-de-sacs of detached homes and townhouses unfurling from wide roads (albeit lined with walking trails). Sprawling shopping plazas and office parks superseded the dense, mixed-use village. Funnily enough, though, when Gulf Reston tried to calculate the most profitable future course for the town, its hulking first-generation computer spat out numbers that affirmed Simon's basic thinking. Gulf and Mobil changed *what* got built. But they didn't deviate far from the original plan in terms of *where* it went. Reston turned out to be a forerunner of common-interest developments, or CIDs, the townhouse and condominium complexes that spread all over American suburbia in the 1960s and 1970s as developers tried to fit more housing units onto ever-more-expensive parcels of fringe land.

Assessing Reston's success is complicated, but the seven goals are a good place to start, and Reston has mostly delivered on them. It has a high proportion of cultural and recreational facilities per capita. It has a range of housing options for all income levels—almost. It features 1,300 acres of open space, including woodlands, wetlands, meadows, streams, and four lakes. As for beauty—another Simon principle—Reston has a robust public-art program and some excellent architecture, and not just from the '60s; one recent addition is a striking, X-gridded building by the Chicago architect Helmut Jahn. Low-cost housing is scarce. But if she can afford to, a person can live and work in Reston, as Simon had hoped. In fact, Reston has succeeded almost too well at avoiding the fate of the bedroom suburb, with 2.5 jobs for every household, many of them in information technology and government contracting. The building of the Dulles Toll Road and its extension to I-66 in the mid-1980s kicked off a long boom in office development by high-tech companies, as that industry began to rise. Simon's instinct that the isolated Bowman farm was a good location turned out to be correct.

———————

Restonians were so stunned by Simon's ouster that some burned their Gulf credit cards. It was a wake-up call: They had bought into Simon's dream of an egalitarian and beautiful alternative to suburbia, and moved there trusting that he would realize it over time. Now, the onus fell on them. Newly minted activists founded a citizens' group, the Reston Community Association, as a counterweight to the suits at Gulf. Then they started building the town's civic institutions, a process that had begun but languished under Simon.

The "pioneers" who settled Reston and other 1960s New Towns were similar to other residents of brand-new suburbs in that they had stepped into a civic vacuum, which they sought to remedy by forming voluntary associations. But a critical difference from the average tract suburb, writes the historian Nicholas Dagen Bloom, was that many Restonians shared "ideals that extended beyond property values, local suburban issues, and domestic tranquility." And the vacuum often worked in their favor. "[T]he liberal residents who favored the new-town ideals gained power quickly because they did not have to fight an established political hierarchy." However, they did have to contend with the developers and the quasi-governmental body of the Reston Association, which the developers controlled until 1985.

One of the most energetic early activists was Embry Rucker, a left-wing Episcopal priest from Kentucky. Rucker had arrived in Reston in 1969 with "some definite ideas," as he wrote in his memoir: He was not going to get sucked into the construction of a new building for his church or fret over money-raising and membership numbers. Instead, he hoped that members of his flock—committed and casual alike—would "become involved in social and political action, not church organization games." Through his Common Ground Foundation, Rucker initiated a flurry of community services in Reston, including a local bus route (using a cast-off van from a canceled jitney service in downtown D.C.), a child-care center that operated above the Safeway in Lake Anne, a hang-out for teenagers called the Rathskeller, a babysitting referral service, a job placement office, and a network of nurses who made house calls.

The year that Rucker appeared on the scene, 1969, also saw the first Reston Black Arts festival, organized by a group of black residents called Reston Black Focus. "We pulled together and we brought some of the social constructs that the black community has—like sororities and social organizations—into the [Reston] community to support other black people when they came," says Laura Thomas, who was a founding member of Reston Black Focus. "When friends of the people who lived here moved here, because they [had] said, 'It's okay, the Ku Klux Klan is not here,' there was already a structure, and resources so they could more easily integrate."

As Mobil built out the town in the '80s, the company wooed homebuyers with a marketing campaign that emphasized Reston as a warm, family-oriented town, rather than a bold experiment in planning. The population exceeded 45,000 in the mid-'80s. The early pioneers and liberal crusaders merged with more recent arrivals who had chosen Reston for more conventional reasons. But liberal activism didn't sputter out. In an inversion of NIMBY opposition to housing or services for low-income people, in the late '80s, Reston residents successfully lobbied *for* a homeless shelter in their town. (It was named, fittingly, after Embry Rucker.) Helping the needy continues to be a Reston value. Cornerstones, the nonprofit that operates the shelter, is a pillar of the town, with multiple programs to alleviate poverty. It runs a food pantry and owns and subsidizes more than 100 housing units for low-income families.

In 1988, Reston took its second big gamble on urbanity. A quarter-century after Conklin and Rossant had set aside land in the master plan for a town center, Reston broke ground on one. Reston Town Center was one of the earliest developments in the country designed on the principles of New Urbanism, a movement that champions a return to how cities and neighborhoods looked before the automobile age, with tight rectilinear street grids, ground-level shops, and buildings that meet the sidewalk. New Urbanist architecture tends toward the nostalgic, whereas Lake Anne's was avant-garde, and Reston's original plan was far more organic and less orthogonal than is kosher for New Urbanists. Nevertheless, Simon and the early advocates of New Urbanism had the same priorities: to make places that encouraged walking, and that arranged homes, stores, offices, and recreation facilities cheek-by-jowl. (Perhaps that's why Simon was more than a little skeptical of the term "New Urbanism": "[N]ew urbanism is neither new nor urban," he sniffed to *Washingtonian* magazine in 2009.)

Like Reston itself, Town Center, designed by RTKL and Sasaki Associates (Hideo Sasaki's firm), was an audacious project. Buildings of ten and fifteen stories rubbed shoulders on the edges of a large square punctuated by a fountain. Town Center now includes towers of twenty-plus stories. It has hundreds of offices and apartments, restaurants, stores, and a movie theater. Many of the buildings have Postmodernist flourishes, or historicizing details that evoke an early twentieth-century commercial district in a big city. And it does feel legitimately urban—for eight square blocks.

Reston's next big stride toward the urban came more recently, with the arrival of the Washington Metro. Metro's Silver Line connects northwestern Fairfax County to downtown D.C. via Tysons (formerly Tyson's Corner), Falls Church, and Arlington. There is currently one Silver Line station in Reston, on its industrial spine, at the intersection of the Dulles Access Road and the arterial road of Wiehle (pronounced like "Greeley") Avenue. High-rise apartment buildings and office towers have sprung up since the station opened in 2014. That year, the county approved updates to Reston's master plan that would turn Wiehle and two future stops on the Silver Line (Reston Town Center North and Herndon) into dense urban districts. The quarter-mile radii around each station were rezoned for a 50/50 split of residential and non-residential uses. All told, the county green-lighted up to 22,000 new residences, almost nine million square feet of new office space, and significant new hotel and retail space. It's a lot, but only a fraction of what's in store for the spaghetti-road "edge city" of Tysons eight miles to the east, in what has been called "the most ambitious re-urbanization project on Earth."

The Reston Citizens Association opposed the upzoning. At the time of writing, residents are fighting a county proposal to raise the density cap in Reston from thirteen to fifteen people per acre. Nine hundred people packed a public meeting in October 2017. "Jeers and boos rang out when officials began defending the amendments," reported the *Fairfax Times*. Some opponents of the recent measures say they don't oppose development per se, but that it will outpace infrastructure and give short shrift to public space under the county's plan. Others believe the level of development is excessive and will change Reston's character irreparably, detracting from their quality of life.

"I have to say it, 'Reston was so much better as a sleepy bedroom community,'" one commenter wrote on a local blog. "I fear that this place is about to become a big crap hole," wrote another.

"People are so distressed about the level of development going in," Shelley Mastran, a geographer, told me. Mastran lives in Reston and is the board chair of the Reston Historic Trust; we were sitting at a table in the small space in Lake Anne's crescent occupied by the Reston Museum. "Even though," she added, "it was all planned. The master plan was updated through a long, laborious, legitimate process." (The update involved nearly 200 public meetings.) "Then, nobody paid attention, but now they're really paying attention, and they're getting very concerned." I asked Mastran whether it was the pace or the scale of the development that bothered people. "I think both," she replied. "I hear so many people say, 'This isn't the bucolic place we moved to.'"

Despite its unique history, Reston finds itself in the same bind as many prosperous suburbs in the United States today. As companies abandon their suburban office parks for downtown, and as more Americans choose where to live based on where they can walk to, suburban governments know they must urbanize to remain competitive. In suburbs blessed with mass transit like Reston, building new mini-cities around the stations is the obvious fix. It can dramatically increase office and residential space, and if the design is good, it will create a bustling "downtown" that a lot of suburbs have lacked from their inception. But existing residents are often taken aback by the sudden sprouting of twenty-story buildings. They worry about the effect of all those incomers on local schools and parks. They are skeptical that the new households will walk and take transit to get everywhere instead of driving on already-clogged streets. And they want trees, not towers, to define the landscape around them.

In Reston, the problem has a twist: This suburb had a revered founder, who explicitly set out his long-term vision, and who moved back to Reston in 1993. (He died in 2015, at age 100.) Simon said in the early 1960s that Reston would reach 75,000 people—by that measure, the town still has room to grow. His construction of the sixteen-story Heron House shows that tall buildings were part of Reston's DNA from the beginning. You can look at the 1962 master plan and Simon's seven goals and find justifications for Fairfax County's aggressive growth plan. A more urban Reston would broaden the range of housing options, as Simon wanted, and it would allow more people to live and work in the same community. Simon "was totally unafraid of density," says Veatch, who became close to his former boss in Simon's later years.

However, Restonians can (and do) cite Simon and the original master plan to make the case against certain kinds of growth. Although he embraced density and urbanity, Simon "was very much in favor of making sure that public transportation and infrastructure was in place to handle that density," Veatch said. The revised master plan would put more intense development not just near the Metro stations but also around Reston's five village centers, which, after Simon was pushed out, were developed as ordinary low-rise shopping centers.

A *Washington Post* article from April 2018 captures the divide in Reston. A local activist named Tammi Petrine told the *Post*, "We are a suburb, and we want to stay a suburb." She elaborated: "If you really think you want to be in a really dense, urbanized community, please move there. We are not that." Petrine leads the group Coalition for a Planned Reston, which wants Fairfax County to scale back development plans around Reston's village centers and put a cap on the population, requests the county has so far denied. On the other side is Canaan Merchant, a Reston resident who contributes to the pro-growth urbanist blog *Greater Greater Washington*. Merchant, the *Post* reported, "was attracted to the area in part because there were enough transportation options that his family didn't need to have a second car," and "likes the idea of a more walkable Reston."

Still, Restonians say the town has a spirit that other places can't match. "There really is a stronger sense of community," says Mastran, who grew up nearby in Hollin Hills and has lived in a number of other suburbs in northern Virginia. "Even though we're not incorporated, people have just a real sense of this being a special place, and taking care of it, in a way." Mastran speculates that the governance structure is responsible for that, in part. The Reston

Association is a hybrid of HOA and conservation trust; residents pay dues to use the swimming pools and tennis courts, but those dues also go to maintaining common areas and protecting natural resources. "There's something about that maybe that helps convey that sense of ownership—of stewardship of place," Mastran notes.

The town that advertised itself as an open community prior to the Fair Housing Act is now more diverse than its founder could have imagined: 63 percent white, 13 percent Hispanic or Latino, 11 percent Asian, and 10 percent black. Five decades after her skeptical back-woods drive to see a model home, Laura Thomas and her husband Carol still live in Reston, now in the Town Center. The Thomases' son Paul has stayed in Reston, too; over the years he has sat on the boards of the Historic Trust, the RA, and the Reston Community Center. Paul and his wife Heather are raising a third generation of Restonians. "Whatever Simon did, whatever the message was, however he advertised it—I can't put my finger on it," Laura Thomas told me. "He attracted people who were very different ethnically and socioeconomically. But they had a commonality of point of view about people. And that became the pervasive thing in Reston."

In the twenty-first century, large urban areas will look less like tree rings—with progressively denser neighborhoods surrounding the "bull's eye" of downtown, the so-called Burgess model—and more like constellations, with multiple mini-cities linked to one another via transit lines across swaths of lower-rise suburbia. This model is known as polycentric urbanization. Reston is a moderately big star in the Washington constellation, and as Restonians grapple with whether their town will be urban or suburban in twenty years, the answer probably lies somewhere in between. "It may be that we're just going to be a little bit like Arlington," Mastran said, referring to an inner suburb of Washington that's known for its smart-growth planning. "There is the Ballston-Rosslyn corridor [in Arlington], and you can live at Ballston or Rosslyn and not have a car, or have only one car, and really live your life in an urban way. Take the Metro to D.C. to work, hang out in the restaurants and bars and the sports facilities that are right there in the corridor, and be perfectly happy. Whereas two blocks away, four blocks away from the Ballston-Rosslyn corridor, it's totally suburban. I could see Reston being like that."

However, if the Washington area continues to be a magnet for high-skilled industries, Reston's very affluence could threaten the socioeconomic diversity that the pioneers prized. With a median household income of $111,000, and median rent approaching $1,700, just keeping, let alone adding, affordable housing is a challenge. The new units going in near the Metro should help in the long term, but right now, their price tags raise eyebrows—and concerns. Inclusive growth is one of the major challenges facing suburbs as they adapt to a post-suburban future. Getting it right means the difference between a place that continues to welcome all sorts of people, and a place that pushes away all but the well-educated and high-earning.

It seems clear which future Bob Simon would have preferred. In his old age, every day, he took the elevator down from his Heron House apartment and walked around the lake and the plaza he had built. Passersby wished him good morning or stopped to chat, and he fed off these little interactions. "At one extreme you have the hermit, and he gets his kicks out of solitude," Simon told an interviewer in his late nineties. "I'm anti-hermit. I get my kicks out of people." Today, the futuristic planning trend is for "smart cities" kitted out with gadgets and sensors, but Simon had the right idea: what we really need is for cities (and suburbs) to be humane.

Photograph by Marion Post Wolcott/Library of Congress

CONCLUSION

Recently, I moved with my family into an archetypal "little box"—a small 1950s rambler, in Silver Spring, Maryland, one mile down the road from the Garden City-inspired condo complex we lived in before. A selling point for me (though for few other buyers, I expect) was the view from the kitchen. Our house backs onto a row of houses designed by Charles Goodman, elegant rectangles of glass and wood that glow like lanterns at night. In the last years of his life, when Goodman was housebound and used an oxygen tank, an architect named Gregory Hunt interviewed him extensively. Goodman expressed disappointment that his work had not had a wide enough impact. "One of the things Goodman lamented was that there weren't more Hollin Hills," Hunt told the *Washington City Paper*. "He said, 'I don't understand why. I can't figure out why.'"

I think about that sometimes when I am pulling weeds or washing dishes. Why didn't Goodman's vision, or the vision of the other designers and planners in this book, gain more purchase? First and foremost, building places a little differently and a little better—departing from standard formulas and spending more on public amenities and high-quality design—is never going to be the easiest or most profitable course. Greenbelt and Reston required enormous initial outlays of capital. Morris Milgram was very nearly defeated in his search for financing, something that TAC members and their friends also struggled with. Yet these communities did avoid financial failure. Reston likely broke even for Mobil in the end, and has prospered since. Milgram turned a small profit; Moon Hill and Five Fields homeowners saw their homes appreciate. From a different perspective, you could say these projects flouted the culture of privatism and the majority's preference for the single-family-home. But how innate is that preference, really? Even the late-nineteenth-century moralizing against apartments was a response to the *rise* of apartment and boardinghouse living among the urban middle class. Single-family homes may dominate suburbia today, but people can only buy what's available, and what's available is largely a holdover from FHA mandates of the 1930s.

Today, segregation by race and class is turning the hinterlands of many cities into patchwork quilts of white and brown, haves and have-nots. Affluent whites often sort themselves into the neighborhoods with the best public schools and the highest, most stable property values. Surrounding these neighborhoods is a force field that prevents change: exclusionary zoning. By banishing lower-cost housing from the area, incumbent homeowners push less advantaged people—who are often not white—to neighborhoods with worse schools, worse access to jobs, fewer parks and stores and services. In some parts of the country, balkanization has gone into warp speed, and once-diverse suburban counties are fracturing into new, smaller, homogeneous municipalities. My *CityLab* colleague Brentin Mock has reported on this in metropolitan Atlanta, where at least ten cities have formed in recent years—a "series of Brexits," in Mock's words, led by white residents. "Now in DeKalb County, the wealthiest and whitest neighborhoods have already decamped, leaving the rest of the county holding the bag, and with less tax revenue to pay for it," he writes.

Enclaveism—the desire to cluster with people who are similar to you—is a thread running through this book. It was a driving force in Economy, Stelton, and in Lexington, and to a lesser degree in Greenbelt, Concord Park, and Reston. It can't be social-engineered away. And it does have real benefits: social cohesion (providing a network of support beyond the nuclear family), high levels of community engagement, and often, a more economical, efficient, and fair use of space and goods, through the trading of private space or privileges for a robust commons. The drawback is that insularity can harden into "not-in-my-back-yard" exclusion, and that needs to be countered. Local governments, by amending their zoning laws to allow duplexes, triplexes, accessory dwelling units, in-home businesses and corner stores, and small apartment buildings, and by rescinding outdated parking requirements, could make a big dent in inequality. Free-wheeling Stelton serves as a good model for more conservative suburbs where people want government to have a light hand. Where a more active role for government is welcomed, municipalities can foster community land trusts, co-housing, and "missing middle" housing through grants, tax breaks, design competitions, and other means. Suburban governments could also promote or maintain integration by building on the work of the Oak Park Housing Center.

As well as spatial segregation, there is the pressing, no-longer-abstract threat of climate change, Again, smart-growth land use and residential design would make a tremendous impact, reducing the car miles that are a major contributor to greenhouse gases, as well as cutting home heating and cooling costs (through smaller housing units) and water use (through lawn alternatives such as shared plazas) Electric vehicles could help mitigate suburbia's climate impacts, but expanding public transportation will be critical to get the level of greenhouse-gas reduction we need. On a faster time scale, roads can be redesigned quickly to promote walking and biking over driving. It's true that suburban neighborhood design, with its inward-looking subdivisions and meandering, dead-end streets, poses a challenge for improving connectivity. But suburbs may actually have more latent potential for sustainability than people assume, since two- and three-story apartment and condo complexes along major roads are quite common. The architect Nico Larco has shown that simple design changes to connect these developments to nearby commercial areas made residents more than 60 percent more likely to walk rather than drive there.

Rather than pushing new development (however well-designed) ever outward, forward-thinking suburbs should try to rejuvenate "grayfields" instead—dead malls, aging commercial strips, and high-vacancy office parks. In Annandale, Virginia, enterprising restaurateurs recently turned a store in a frayed strip mall into a popular Asian food court called The Block, simply giving it a fresh coat of paint, new signage, and an interior remodel. Twenty miles away in Rockville, Maryland, a neighborhood association collaborated with county planners in 2018 to put on a "placemaking festival" in a large shopping-center parking lot. Over a few days, they striped the asphalt with colorful paint, built a bandshell and picnic tables, and set up stations like a mini-library and hula-hoop area. More than 1,000 people attended, and Montgomery County planner Atul Sharma immediately started getting phone calls from other civic associations: "They're all asking for the same thing," he told me. Not every suburban municipality has the means to spur redevelopment or the population growth to warrant it. In some places, turning "grayfields" into parks, community gardens, or wetlands makes more sense.

Even if local officials and community leaders are proactive, there is the problem of *private* government, which is ubiquitous in American suburbia. HOAs and condos are extremely difficult to dissolve or reform. When suburban jurisdictions relax their zoning and plan new transit initiatives, activists may have to plot cul-de-sac coups to take over their HOA and condo boards and get them behind the efforts. If they are really ambitious, they could try to amend bylaws that (for instance) exclude renter representation on the board, prohibit homeowners from taking in boarders and building ADUs, and micromanage the use and appearance of front yards.

Whether or not they live under a private government, suburban residents need to stand up for social and racial equity, walking, cycling and mass transit, and more housing options. My hope is that this book will inspire suburban readers to dig into their local history as well. The myth of modern suburbia is that it sprang up on freshly bulldozed cropland, but many suburbs are palimpsests of successive communities that have been forgotten—especially if they were informal and/or non-white communities. A lot of suburban history no doubt remains to be written.

In the process of researching this book, I picked up a folder in the archives of the Reston Historic Trust and opened it to find photos of three notable people of the 1960s standing outdoors together and talking: Bob Simon; HUD's first secretary, Robert Weaver; and the great writer on cities, Jane Jacobs. They were in Reston, and as a letter in the folder explained, they were watching the "inflation" of a concrete dome by a visiting Italian architect. (It didn't work, although apparently the dome stayed up on a subsequent trial at Columbia University.)

How had the Italian architect ended up in Reston? What was Jacobs, who was sharply critical of the suburbs, doing there? Perhaps Simon admired her writing and was trying to win her over, as he had with Mumford. My inquiries brought few answers. But I kept thinking about those photos. A maverick developer, the first African-American cabinet member in U.S. history, and the writer who changed how we thought about cities, watching an architectural experiment unfold inside a bigger architectural experiment. We can't let that sense of possibility slip away. As the founders of Stelton knew, trudging through the rain to their new home, and the Concord Park residents who stood vigil over the Myers' house in Levittown: Suburbia is what we make it.

SOURCES

INTRODUCTION

Angel, Shlomo. *Planet of Cities*. Cambridge, Massachusetts: Lincoln Institute of Land Policy, 2012.

Crawford, Margaret. "Little Boxes: High-Tech and the Silicon Valley." *Room One Thousand*, Issue 1 (2013).

Dunham-Jones, Ellen, and Williamson, June. *Retrofitting Suburbia: Urban Design Solutions for Redesigning Suburbs*. Hoboken, New Jersey: John Wiley & Sons, 2009.

Fishman, Robert. *Bourgeois Utopias: The Rise and Fall of Suburbia*. New York: Basic Books, 1989.

Forsyth, Ann. "Defining Suburbs." *Journal of Planning Literature* 27, no. 3 (2012).

Hayden, Dolores. *Building Suburbia: Green Fields and Urban Growth, 1820–2000*. New York: Vintage Books, 2004.

Intergovernmental Panel on Climate Change. "Summary for Policymakers of IPCC Special Report on Global Warming of 1.5°C approved by governments." October 8, 2018.

Jackson, Kenneth T. *Crabgrass Frontier: The Suburbanization of the United States*. New York and Oxford: Oxford University Press, 1985.

Keil, Roger. *Suburban Planet: Making the World Urban from the Outside In*. Cambridge, UK and Medford, Massachusetts: Polity Books, 2018.

Kolko, Jed. "How Suburban Are Big American Cities?" *FiveThirtyEight*, May 21, 2015.

Krier, Léon, "The City Within a City." *A+U* Special Issue (1977).

Lacapra, Véronique. "Ancient Suburb Near St. Louis Could Be Lost Forever." *NPR*, May 25, 2012.

Merriman, John M. *The Margins of City Life: Explorations on the French Urban Frontier, 1815–1851*. New York and Oxford: Oxford University Press, 1991.

Montgomery, David, and Florida, Richard. "How the Suburbs Will Swing the Midterm Election." *CityLab*, October 5, 2018.

National Association of Realtors. "Millennials Favor Walkable Communities, Says New NAR Poll." July 28, 2015.

New Urbanist Memes for Transit-Oriented Teens. Timeline [Facebook group].

Nicolaides, Becky M., and Wiese, Andrew, eds. *The Suburb Reader*. First Edition. New York and Abingdon, UK: Routledge, 2006.

Schneider, Carrie. "Vital Suburbia: An Interview With Charles Renfro by Carrie Schneider." *OffCite*, July 17, 2014.

Sellers, Christopher C. *Crabgrass Crucible: Suburban Nature and the Rise of Environmentalism in Twentieth-Century America*. Chapel Hill: University of North Carolina Press, 2012.

Vaughan, Laura, ed. *Suburban Urbanities: Suburbs and the Life of the High Street*. London: UCL Press, 2015.

Wiese, Andrew. *Places of Their Own: African American Suburbanization in the Twentieth Century*. Chicago and London: University of Chicago Press, 2005.

Wright, Gwendolyn. *Building the Dream: A Social History of Housing in America*. Cambridge, Massachusetts and London: MIT Press, 1983.

CHAPTER 1

Arndt, Karl J.R. *George Rapp's Harmony Society, 1785-1847*. Philadelphia: University of Pennsylvania Press, 1965.

Bentley, Chris. "Can Boomers Make Cohousing Mainstream?" *CityLab*, January 20, 2015.

"Economy National Historic Landmark." National Register of Historic Places Inventory–Nomination Form (1986).

Lewis, Michael J. *City of Refuge: Separatists and Utopian Town Planning*. Princeton and Oxford: Princeton University Press, 2016.

Martin, Courtney E. "Modern Housing With Village Virtues." *The New York Times*, September 20, 2016.

Nordhoff, Charles. *The Communistic Societies of the United States*. New York: Harper & Brothers, 1875.

Pittsburgh Music History: John Duss. [Webpage.] Accessed at https://sites.google.com/site/pittsburghmusichistory/pittsburgh-music-story/classic/john-duss.

Pitzer, Donald E., ed. *America's Communal Utopias.* Chapel Hill and London: University of North Carolina Press, 1997.

Tady, Scott. "Ambridge Historic District is hopping; could it someday be hip?" *The Beaver County Times,* June 4, 2018.

Versluis, Arthur. "Western Esotericism and the Harmony Society." *Esoterica* I (1999).

CHAPTER 2

Arms, Louis Lee. "An Anarchist Colony 70 Minutes From Broadway." *The New York Tribune,* September 14, 1919.

Avrich, Paul. *The Modern School Movement: Anarchism and Education in the United States.* Edinburgh and Oakland, West Virginia: AK Press, 2006.

Buchan, Perdita. *Utopia, New Jersey: Travels in the Nearest Eden.* New Brunswick and London: Rivergate Books, 2007.

Kahlenberg, Richard. "Taking on Class and Racial Discrimination in Housing." *The American Prospect,* August 4, 2018.

Scott, Jon Thoreau, ed. *Recollections From the Modern School Ferrer Colony.* Altamont, New York: The Friends of the Modern School, 2007.

Veysey, Laurence. *The Communal Experience: Anarchist & Mystical Communities in Twentieth-Century America*. Chicago and London: University of Chicago Press, 1978.

CHAPTER 3

"American Housing: A Failure, a Problem, a Potential Boon and Boom." *Life*, November 15, 1937.

Arnold, Joseph L. *The New Deal in the Suburbs: A History of the Greenbelt Town Program, 1935-1954*. Columbus: Ohio University Press, 1971.

Bauer, Catherine. "The dreary deadlock of public housing." *Architectural Forum* (May 1957). Republished by *Places Journal* (October 2018) as "The (Still) Dreary Deadlock of Public Housing."

Dreier, Peter. "Why America Needs More Social Housing." *The American Prospect*, Spring 2018.

"Eyes on Greenbelt." *The Washington Post*, September 3, 1937.

Gournay, Isabelle, and Sies, Mary Corbin. "Greenbelt, Maryland: Beyond the Iconic Legacy." In Longstreth, Richard (ed.), *Housing Washington: Two Centuries of Residential Development and Planning in the National Capital Area*. Chicago: Center for American Places, 2010.

Green, Jean. "'Kitchen of Future' Discovered in Model Houses in Greenbelt." *The Washington Post*, September 16, 1937.

"Greenbelt, Maryland Historic District." National Historic Landmark Nomination (n.d.).

"Greenbelt Towns: A Demonstration in Suburban Planning." Washington, D.C.: Resettlement Administration, September 1936.

Hurley, Amanda Kolson. "Will US Cities Design Their Way Out of the Affordable Housing Crisis?" *Next City*, January 18, 2016.

Knepper, Cathy D. *Greenbelt, Maryland: A Living Legacy of the New Deal*. Baltimore and London: Johns Hopkins University Press, 2001.

McKenzie, Evan. *Privatopia: Homeowner Associations and the Rise of Residential Private Government*. New Haven and London: Yale University Press, 1994.

Olson, Sidney. "President Likes 'Tugwelltown,' Fishes and All." *The Washington Post*, November 14, 1936.

Reblando, Jason. *New Deal Utopias*. Heidelberg and Berlin: Kehrer, 2017.

Sage Policy Group. "An Economic Development Strategy for Greenbelt, MD" (December 2014).

Stein, Clarence S. *Toward New Towns for America*. Cambridge, Massachusetts and London: MIT Press, 1966.

Steiner, Ralph, and Van Dyke, Willard, dir. *The City*. 1939.

Sternsher, Bernard. *Rexford Tugwell and the New Deal*. New Brunswick and London: Rutgers University Press, 1964.

Von Hoffman, Alexander. "History lessons for today's housing policy: the politics of low-income housing." *Housing Policy Debate*, 22:3 (June 2012).

Warner, George A. *Greenbelt: The Cooperative Community—An Experience in Democratic Living*. New York: Exposition Press, 1954.

Wood, Edith Elmer. *The Housing of the Unskilled Wage Earner: America's Next Problem*. New York: Macmillan, 1919.

CHAPTER 4

Adams, Annmarie. "The Eichler Home: Intention and Experience in Postwar Suburbia." *Perspectives in Vernacular Architecture*, Vol. 5 (1995).

Five Fields - Five Decades: A Community in Progress. Lexington, Massachusetts: Five Fields Inc., 2001.

Fixler, David. "Hipsters in the Woods: The Midcentury-Modern Suburban Development," *Architecture Boston* (Spring 2009).

Hyde, Rory. "What Would Boyd Do? A Small Homes Service for Today," *Architecture Australia* (May 2018, Issue 3).

Kubo, Michael. *Architecture Incorporated: Authorship, Anonymity, and Collaboration in Postwar Modernism*. Massachusetts Institute of Technology doctoral thesis, 2017.

Kubo, Michael. "The Cambridge School: What went on at 46 Brattle Street," *Architecture Boston* (Summer 2013).

"Mid-Century Modern Houses of Lexington, Massachusetts." National Register of Historic Places Multiple Property Documentation Form (2012).

Moon Hill Memories: 50th Anniversary, June 14th, 1997. Lexington, Massachusetts: Six Moon Hill, 1997.

Oshima, Ken Tadashi. "Building Utopia at Six Moon Hill: The Fletcher House." *A+U* (1997).

"Six Moon Hill: Collaborative planning integrates tailor-made houses in co-op subdivision, demonstrates new ideas in design." *Architectural Forum* 92 (June 1950).

"Six Moon Hill Historic District." National Register of Historic Places Registration Form (n.d.).

"The Good Life, Inc." *Vogue*, February 1954.

Walker, Barbara. "No Woman Should Stay Home." *The Boston Globe*, March 2, 1947.

CHAPTER 5

Badger, Emily. "A radical idea to compensate black homeowners harmed by racial bias." *The Washington Post*, June 21, 2016.

Breymaier, J. Robert. "The Social and Economic Value of Intentional Integration Programs in Oak Park, IL." Joint Center for Housing Studies of Harvard University, 2017.

"Greenbelt Knoll." Philadelphia Register of Historic Places (2006).

Grier, Eunice S. and George W. *Privately Developed Interracial Housing: An Analysis of Experience*. Berkeley and Los Angeles: University of California Press, 1960.

Milgram, Morris. *Good Neighborhood: The Challenge of Open Housing*. New York: W.W. Norton, 1979.

Pigott, W. Benjamin. "The 'Problem' of the Black Middle Class: Morris Milgram's Concord Park and Residential Integration in Philadelphia's Postwar Suburbs." *Pennsylvania Magazine of History and Biography*, Vol. 132, No. 2 (April 2008).

Rosen, Harry M. and David H. *But Not Next Door*. New York: Avon, 1962.

Rothstein, Richard. *The Color of Law: A Forgotten History of How Our Government Segregated America*. New York and London: Liveright, 2017.

Sugrue, Thomas J. *Sweet Land of Liberty: The Forgotten Struggle for Civil Rights in the North*. New York: Random House, 2008.

CHAPTER 6

Aratani, Lori. "Metro's Silver Line ushers in a new age for Reston, leaving residents divided." *The Washington Post*, April 22, 2018.

Bloom, Nicholas Dagen. *Suburban Alchemy: 1960s New Towns and the Transformation of the American Dream.* Columbus: Ohio State University Press, 2001.

Bose, Alec. "Raising the roof in Reston." *The Fairfax County Times*, October 27, 2017.

Goff, Karen. "Reston Founder Robert E. Simon Dies at 101." *Reston Now*, September 21, 2015.

Grubisich, Tom, and McCandless, Peter. *Reston: The First Twenty Years.* Reston: Reston Publishing Company, 1985.

Huxtable, Ada Louise. "A Crucial Test for American Town Planning." *The New York Times*, September 25, 1967.

Huxtable, Ada Louise. "'Clusters' Instead of 'Slurbs.'" *The New York Times*, February 9, 1964.

Huxtable, Ada Louise. "Fully Planned Town Opens in Virginia." *The New York Times*, December 5, 1965.

"Lake Anne Village Center Historic District." National Register of Historic Places Registration Form (2017).

Lindsay, Drew. "What I've Learned: Pioneer of the Suburbs." *Washingtonian*, November 1, 2009.

McFadden, Robert D. "Robert E. Simon Jr., Who Created a Town, Reston, Va., Dies at 101." *The New York Times*, September 21, 2015.

McLeod, Ethan. "Board of Supervisors Approves Reston Master Plan." *Reston Connection*, February 20, 2014.

Neibauer, Michael. "Fairfax board adopts new Reston vision, possibly doubling development." *Washington Business Journal*, February 11, 2014.

Novak, Matt. "The Late Great American Promise of Less Work." *Gizmodo*, April 10, 2014.

O'Connell, Jonathan. "Robert E. Simon: Advocate for smart growth 50 years before its time." *The Washington Post*, April 8, 2012.

"Op-Ed: Are We Reston? Or Rosslyn?" *Reston Now*, February 9, 2018.

Reston Association: PRC Zoning Amendment. [Webpage.] Accessed at http://www.reston.org/ DevelopmentFutureofReston/PRCZoningAmendment/ tabid/1038/Default.aspx

"RCA Gives Reston Master Plan Draft a Solid 'D,' Plans to Oppose It." Restonian.org, October 29, 2013.

"Resistance is futile?" *Reston Connection*, August 15, 2006.

"Reston, VA: New Design for an Ideal City." *Ebony*, December 1966.

"Robert E. Simon Jr.'s suburban success story." *The Washington Post*, September 22, 2015.

Somashekhar, Sandhya. "The Oft-Imitated Reston Eyes Future With Trepidation." *The Washington Post*, November 28, 2008.

Wingert-Jabi, Rebekah, dir. *Another Way of Living: The Story of Reston, VA*. 2015.

CONCLUSION

Larco, Nico, Kelsey, Kristin, and West, Amanda. *Site Design for Multifamily Housing: Creating Livable, Connected Neighborhoods*. Washington, D.C., Covelo, and London: Island Press, 2014.

Mock, Brentin. "Atlanta: A Tale of New Cities." *CityLab*, March 10, 2018.

Morton, David. "Heart of Glass." *Washington City Paper*, September 5, 2003.

ACKNOWLEDGMENTS

Thank you to Anne Trubek, who believed in this project and took a chance on a bare-bones proposal. I'll always be grateful. Belt's Dan Crissman made deft and sensitive edits to the manuscript, and Meredith Pangrace turned it into a good-looking book. Michelle Blankenship helped get the word out.

A special thanks is due to fellow writers and experts who took time to comment on chapter drafts, improving them immensely: Richard Florida, Daniel Kay Hertz, Alexandra Lange, Fernanda Perrone, and Jason Reblando. My colleagues at *CityLab* cheered me on and inspired me throughout the writing process. Before I joined *CityLab*, editors at other publications helped clarify my thinking on suburban issues: Sudip Bose, Ariella Cohen, Nancy Levinson, Annys Shin, and Eric Wills. My virtual circle of friends on Twitter also offered countless tips and insights. Michael Kubo kindly shared some of his doctoral research on The Architects Collaborative. Elizabeth Evitts Dickinson and Fred Scharmen were early supporters and sounding boards.

I could not have written this book without the generous help of the historians, archivists, community activists, and museum directors I met during the course of my research—and most of all, the wonderful residents of the communities profiled in these pages. My heartfelt thanks go to Jason Beske, Rob Breymaier, Sarah Buffington, Alexandra Campbell, Leo Goldman, Isabelle Gournay, Joyce Hadley, David Hovde, Alexander Khost, Shelley Mastran, Daryl McCurdy, Gene Milgram, Laurelyn Roberts, Jon Thoreau Scott, Lauren Swann, Laura Thomas, Rick Treitman, Chuck Veatch, Rebekah Wingert-Jabi, and Megan Searing Young.

The idea for the book emerged as I read important scholarship on suburbia, new and old (but especially new). I owe a substantial intellectual debt to Margaret Crawford, Ann Forsyth, Richard Harris, Willow Lung-Amam, Becky Nicolaides, Andrew Wiese, June Williamson, and other scholars who have done much to dispel the conventional wisdom about suburbs. The seed of this project was planted in 2013, when I met Roger Keil on a visit to Toronto's suburbs while reporting a feature article for *Next City*. Thanks, Roger.

Most of all, I am grateful to my family and friends for their patient support over the past two years. Especially Lawrence and Nick—my favorite suburbanites. *Radical Suburbs* is dedicated to my father, Ken Kolson, who shaped the writer and person I became in ways too deep to fathom.